Public Journalism and Public Life

Why Telling the News Is Not Enough
Second Edition

LEA'S COMMUNICATION SERIES
Jennings Bryant/Dolf Zillmann, General Editors

Selected titles in Journalism (Maxwell McCombs, Advisory Editor) include:

Fensch • The Sports Writing Handbook, Second Edition

Garrison • Computer-Assisted Reporting

Garrison • Professional Feature Writing, Second Edition

Lacy/Sohn/Wicks • Media Management: A Casebook Approach

Weaver/Wilhoit • The American Journalist in the 1990s:
U.S. News People at the End of an Era

DeWerth-Pallmeyer • The Audience in the News

Black • Mixed News: The Public/Civic/Communitarian/Journalism Debate

For a complete list of other titles in LEA's Communication Series, please contact Lawrence Erlbaum Associates, Publishers.

Public Journalism and Public Life

Why Telling the News Is Not Enough
Second Edition

Davis "Buzz" Merritt

LEA LAWRENCE ERLBAUM ASSOCIATES, PUBLISHERS
1998 Mahwah, New Jersey   London

Lawrence Erlbaum Associates, Inc., Publishers
10 Industrial Avenue
Mahwah, New Jersey 07430

Cover design by Kathryn Houghtaling

Library of Congress Cataloging-in-Publication Data

Merritt, Davis.
    Public journalism and public life : why telling the news
is not enough / Davis Merritt. —2nd ed.
        p.   cm.
    Includes bibliographical references (p.) and index.
    ISBN 0-8058-2707-2 (cloth : alk. paper)—ISBN 0-8058-
2708-0 (pbk. : alk. paper)
    1. Journalistic ethics.   2. Journalism—Objectivity.   I.
Title.
PN4756.M3855   1997
174'.9097—dc21   97-15069
                                                                CIP

Books published by Lawrence Erlbaum Associates are printed
on acid-free paper, and their bindings are chosen for strength
and durability.

Printed in the United States of America
10   9   8   7   6   5   4   3   2   1

*To Libby, who has lived all of this with me
and whose wisdom always makes the peaks higher
and the valleys less deep.*

Contents

Preface to the
Second Edition

In late 1994, as I was winding up the first edition of this book, I joined my friend Balbir Mathur for one of our occasional lunches. Balbir, a native of India and a successful American entrepreneur, has spent the last decade on a modest personal quest: relieving world hunger. His classically entrepreneurial approach is a combination of Eastern vision and hard-nosed Western incentive. His charitable organization, Trees for Life Inc., has planted millions of fruit trees in underdeveloped countries and provided materials to teach people in those countries how to use the trees for food, building and clothing materials, and income. It is a rolling revolution in self-help.

He was aware of my quest, 4 years at that point, to try to change the nature of journalism, and after we ordered lunch he asked, "How's it going?"

"Fine," I said.

"You've been at this for 3 or 4 years. Are you seeing any progress?"

"Oh, yeah," I said. "There's ... "

"That's too bad," he interjected.

"What do you mean, Balbir?"

"If this is important change," he said softly, "if it's really fundamental and you've been at it only 3 or 4 years and think you're seeing progress, then you're not asking all the right questions and you're not looking in all the right places."

As I write this in early 1997, I understand in ways I could not have understood on that day the wisdom of his advice, and I relate the story here to underscore the point he made.

When the idea of public journalism began to be discussed broadly in the profession in the years after 1994, it was blindsided by the quintessentially modern American demand for instant results. I deal with the effects of that unrewarding phenomenon in chapter 10, but for now simply note that, 7 years into this quest, real but quiet progress is being made.

In part, progress is occurring because the initial and misdirected condemnation of the idea is giving way to a more thoughtful consideration by many journalists. The ostensible heavy hitters in the profession's elite instantly and almost unanimously attacked the idea, often without attempting to understand it. Even in the face of those outraged and sometimes outrageous protestations, the idea did not wilt. Like Balbir with his trees, I see my task as planting seeds that will produce fruit only over time and many seasons, including some harsh winters.

Public journalism involves cultural change of a fundamental nature. The culture in which we have operated took decades to develop and will require decades to change. This second edition expands and further develops the basic philosophy set out in the first edition and also takes into account questions and challenges that have arisen in the first years of the profession's debate over it. Although this second edition offers accumulated experience and idea development and includes some concrete suggestions, the fundamentals are still as expressed in the first edition's preface and introduction, portions of which follow.

This is about change—in journalism and one journalist—and the need for more of it. It is about the profession that has occupied my life for 4 decades and democracy, and the essential but poorly understood and insufficiently utilized connection between the two.

The needed change is not easy. It is not about journalists doing a few things differently, or doing a few different things. It is fundamental, the adoption of a role beyond telling the news.

I hope to encourage journalists by showing how a new purposefulness can reinvigorate a battered and wandering profession, and to encourage conscientious citizens who are concerned about the viability of public life so that it, too, can be reinvigorated.

These two objectives are equally important and are interwoven: In fact, they are indistinguishable. In a society of increasingly disaffected, cynical, and withdrawn citizens who are flooded with contextless information, effective public life must have shared, relevant information and a place to discuss the implications of that information. Only free and independent journalists can—but usually do not—provide those things. Likewise, effective public life needs the attention and involvement of conscientious citizens, which only they can provide. On the other hand, if people are not interested in public life, they have no need for journalists or journalism.

So this effort addresses the needs and possibilities of both journalism and citizens.

Because I have spent my life in newspapers, the framework is necessarily that of the journalist. But if conscientious citizens as well as journalists can understand the peculiar culture that drives journalists' behavior, they can see the potential for change and help to bring it about.

Two assumptions underlie this book: that public life is not going well, and that journalism as a profession is in trouble with the public for many reasons that can be overcome. If you feel that our democracy is clicking along just fine and are convinced that journalism's future is assured, stop now. Little time and effort will be spent here trying to persuade you otherwise. If, on the other hand, you are concerned about either, you're invited to explore some possibilities for doing something about both.

This second edition is in three segments:

Part I summarizes the arguments of why journalism and public life are inseparably bound in success or failure, and why the way journalism operates in the current environment fosters failure more often than success. The conclusions contained in chapters 1 and 2 grow out of my newspaper experience and observations of public life, and the support for them is detailed in the chapters that follow.

Part II looks at the evolution of the profession's culture, how it acted on one journalist, me, over 4 decades, and how I came to believe that substantive change is needed.

Part III deals with the implications of public journalism philosophy: how it requires the application of additional values to our daily work; how it has evolved in its early years and where it now needs to go; some questions about the cyberspace future; and closing thoughts.

A WORD ABOUT TERMS

The reader will benefit by keeping in mind certain assumptions that underlie these ideas and how certain terms are used.

Public life is the means by which democracy is expressed and experienced. It is not politics alone. Politics is the mechanism by which our constitutional government functions. Public life involves more than that, and includes any activity where people try to achieve common goals or address common problems.

Journalist is used to mean any person who sets out to inform the public about current affairs. It includes newspaper people, broadcasters, article writers of all sorts, and their editors.

Journalism is used as a generic term without reference to its form or delivery system. This is done because the principles discussed are applicable now or in the future, when there will be forms of delivery we cannot conceive of yet. Where the reference is to a particular existing form, that name is used.

The terms *the media* and *the press*, although convenient, are not used to describe journalism or journalists, except, of course, in direct quotations by others. They have become gummy terms, almost of disparagement, in American conversation. The media are more than journalism, including forms and materials—films, non-news television, plays, books, entertainment vehicles—that are not of immediate concern here. The media and the press are commercial endeavors that may or may not include journalism as a part of what they do. The distinction is important. We deal here with the parts of those businesses that involve journalism.

ACKNOWLEDGMENTS

Special appreciation must go first to Jay Rosen, whose encouragement, intellectual direction, and friendship focused and sharpened a restless mind and spirit. And to David Mathews, whose long and patient quest to improve public life provided both a model and a wealth of wisdom.

My gratitude also goes to:

Clark Hoyt of Knight-Ridder Inc. and Reid Ashe, former publisher of *The Wichita Eagle*, for readily endorsing a year's leave in 1994 to reflect upon these matters; Sheri Dill of *The Eagle* for taking on the burden of leading the newspaper for that year; the journalists at *The Eagle* who bore with restraint the sometimes intolerable and unfathomable meanderings of their editor;

Early readers and commentators Vernon Keel, Larry Jinks, Edmund Lambeth, Maxwell McCombs, and Phillip Meyer; to Don Williams for his rare editing touch; and Denis Bruce for research.

A great debt is owed the late James K. Batten, Knight-Ridder Inc.'s chairman and CEO and a friend for 35 years, for establishing a unique professional atmosphere that nurtures creativity and community concern.

And, finally but crucially, thanks to all the quoted authors whose insights made working on this project a journey of personal discovery and reward.

Buzz Merritt

PART I

❖ O N E ❖

Why Change?

Journalists provide a product—news—that is undefined and stubbornly indefinable. We do so without universal, formal rules, without legal prescriptions or proscriptions. We conjure up this product using the lives of people and institutions—their fortunes and reputations—guided only by the sometimes contradictory conventions of a peculiar culture. We employ, under enormous time pressure, the fragile ambiguity of the English language to do all that. And we go home to sleep at night and start all over the next day.

Rarely, if ever, are we allowed the luxury, and burden, of thinking about Teresa Peron, the young Catholic school teacher in screenwriter Kurt Luedtke's remarkable movie *Absence of Malice*. In the film, the fact that Teresa had an abortion is about to be revealed in hundreds of thousands of copies of the Miami newspaper. In the dew of early morning, she sits forlornly on her doorstep. She hears the paperboy working his way down the street, plunking newspapers on the grass. She picks hers up, sees the story, and starts slowly, wearily walking from yard to yard, picking up as many delivered newspapers, one at a time, as she can.

Other people, journalists, had made a decision about her and her life: that her abortion was a reportable detail in a newsworthy situation. The decision was based on axioms about the public's right to know, the First Amendment, objectivity, the public good—the liturgy of journalism's priesthood. The fact that she would kill herself as a result of the story would also be dutifully reported.

The cinema journalists who made the decision that Teresa's privacy was secondary to other considerations did not do so cavalierly. They discussed and agonized and balanced and weighed, but their deliberations began and ended in a culture that values, above all else, making information public; whose prime directive and fundamental urge is disclosure; whose cool and cultivated detachment enables them to separate their actions from the consequences of those actions.

The purpose here is not to debate the merits of that fictional decision, much less any nonfictional ones. Rehashing the handling of specific stories fills the literature of the profession, consumes endless hours at bars favored by journalists, and constitutes much of the formal and informal conversation in newsrooms. Such debates are sometimes useful, but they almost always simply reestablish that journalism is the practice of a human art, not a mechanical science; that even the simplest story involves levels of complexity and human realities, known and unknown. In such an environment, the proper application of rules to circumstance is always endlessly arguable. A news story is, finally, the accumulation of what is seen by the people writing and editing it, the omission of what is not seen, and the accumulated weight of their experiences and beliefs.

Because of that reality, little time will be spent here critiquing how existing canons and rules have been applied in specific stories. Rather, my purpose is to think about the origins of those canons and rules—why we do things—and the possibility that they could and should change; that we might do things differently for different reasons.

JOURNALISM'S ROLE IN DEMOCRACY

Begin with the proposition that public life—the way in which our democracy is expressed and experienced—is not going well. Our formal politics, which is only one part of public life, is sodden and largely ineffective. Many Americans view it as being a world apart from their realities, as already subjected to a hostile takeover by special interests and professional politicians. The other part of public life—our civic ethic—is largely inward-looking, as Americans isolate themselves in their own narrow concerns and seek safety and solace in insular communities and activities.

The gap between citizen and government has grown. Citizens do not trust their governments to properly tend to important matters, but are increasingly less inclined because of the pressures of their personal lives to tend to them themselves.

Meanwhile, the dispiriting list of long-standing national problems such as crime, a lagging educational system, dysfunctional families, and environmental deterioration grows rather than shrinks. Discussions about solutions degenerate into shouting matches across an ideological gap that is a false construct of extremes designed by politicians and perpetuated by journalists. Such false framing leaves citizens little hope for resolution of their problems and, worse, virtually insures that little good can happen. This occurs because the presentation of issues as having only extreme solutions attracts some citizens to one or the other of the poles whereas it convinces others, the majority of whom tend toward the middle ground on most issues, that they and their more moderate views are not and cannot be part of the debate. Either way, true deliberation that can lead to consent about important issues is foreclosed; so the problems persist year after year, decade after decade.

As a result, in the 1980s, a majority of Americans expressed for the first time the opinion that their children would inherit a society less livable, more dangerous, and offering less opportunity than they had. It was an unprecedented negative judgment, far more profound and devastating than mere pessimism.

Not coincidentally, for the first time since 1924, only half of the nation's registered voters bothered to vote for President in 1988, and in 1996 that tragic number fell below half.

Furthermore, in 1994, *The Times-Mirror* Center for the People and *the Press* reported that 71% of Americans agreed with the statement, "The news media gets in the way of society solving its problems." Only 25% agreed that the news media "helps society solve its problems" (p. 178).

Economics formed a part of citizens' unease with the future, but forces less cyclical and more corrosive than a lax economy were at work on the citizens' mind and soul. Various commentators diagnosed the slide toward the precipice from their particular points of view, including a slackening of religious and moral values; government gridlock; the restructuring of traditional family life; the dissolution of community spawned by short-sighted, auto-based sprawl; the yen; the deutsche mark; even vibrations from a rogue comet, still unseen, hurtling toward the earth.

Any one of the dozens or hundreds of theories is as spinnable as any other, for each winds up dealing with only one dimension of a multidimensional problem: Public life—democracy—is not fulfilling its historic promise.

Like other Americans, thoughtful journalists are troubled. Many of the people who entered newspaper journalism in the mid-20th century, and most of those who succeeded at it, shared a vision. Journalism, we sensed, mattered; it was an integral part of the democratic process; it had purpose. That core importance gave substance and meaning to an otherwise low-paying trade.

By 1993, however, one in five working journalists told pollsters that they would probably leave the field within 5 years, a number twice that of figures found in 1982 and 1983 (Weaver & Wilhoit, 1992). These numbers reflect an increasing decline in job satisfaction. Journalism, the respondents are saying, will not matter enough in the future. Its core importance is eroded and its purposefulness lost, making it simply one literary and visual trade among many.

Part of this disillusionment stems from the state in which journalism and the economic structures that support journalism find themselves. By nearly every measure, the journalistic product—newspapers, broadcast news, magazines—is not believed and our motives not trusted. The economic bases, primarily advertising, of the business structures that support journalism are struggling against rapidly expanding competition.

It is no coincidence that the decline in journalism and the decline in public life have happened at the same time. In modern society, they are codependent: Public life needs the information and perspective that journalism can provide, and journalism needs a viable public life because without one, there is no need for journalism.

Thus journalism and the people in the field face a challenge. If we are to leave our country a better place than we found it and secure our profession's future, a great deal must change. This book about journalism and democracy suggests a place to start.

My biases should be understood at the outset. I believe:

- Journalism in all its forms ignores its obligations to effective public life;
- That failure has been a major contributor to the resultant malaise in public life;
- Journalism should be—and can be—a primary force in the revitalization of public life.

However, fundamental change in the profession—cultural, generational change—is necessary for that to occur.

I do not contend that journalists alone can or should be the primary moving force, just as we were not the sole actors in the decline. People in general and politicians in particular were coconspirators. Nor do I suggest that most of present journalistic practice needs to be abandoned. Our modern practices are not so much defective as they are insufficient. The reporting, sorting, and analyzing of news are important functions; they simply are not the only or even the most important ones.

Journalism contains, at least for now, the power either to cultivate or thwart a healthy public life. Without fundamental change within the profession, the latter will continue.

There is, of course, a possible alternative. By remaining on its present insufficient and restricted course, journalism will make itself wholly irrelevant. A society that considers journalism to be only an irritating appurtenance or a negative burden rather than an interested stakeholder will look elsewhere for ways of getting the information necessary for that society to function. The Information Superhighway clearly suggests that possibility, even while offering journalists an opportunity to reestablish the profession's core importance and authority that should be its contribution to public life.

To do this, we must clarify our own values, realize the true context of our work and begin to look at ourselves in a different way. This book thus argues for a redefinition of journalism.

I suggest the revitalization of public life as a broad purpose for journalism and journalists. For no matter the state of individual morals, the efforts of government, the structure of families, the rise or fall of the yen and the deutsche mark, the course of a menacing comet; if public life does not go well, if communities cannot act collectively and effectively to solve problems, Americans' fears about the future will surely be realized. And no matter what we do as journalists, if people are not attentive to public life, if they continue to retreat into only private concerns, they will have no need for journalists or journalism.

Conversely, we can help revitalize public life and restore the core importance to our profession by becoming fair-minded participants in public life rather than detached observers. (*Fair-minded participant* does not mean wholesale involvement in the affairs that we cover. It is a much more limited concept, and is detailed in chapter 8.)

I do not propose a formula; if one exists, it has yet to be discovered. Based on recent trends in journalism, we need to be extremely skeptical of quick fixes that do not involve fundamental change. So this is not a how to manual, it is a *why* discussion. I try to imagine a journalism that is extended—one that has purpose beyond merely telling the news—and an audience that intelligently uses a revitalized journalistic product to help public life go well. How that idea is made concrete depends on the courage and imagination of the wonderfully varied, fiercely independent minds who have chosen journalism as a profession.

My primary purpose is not to try to describe or encourage a particular device or set of practices. To do so would, in itself, limit the possibilities. My objective is to stimulate thoughtful, serious discussion both inside and outside the profession about journalism's true place in a democracy. The aim is not to provide, even if I could, immediate and specific answers. Journalism and public life did not reach their points of present decline quickly, and they will not recover quickly. Those specific answers will have to be found over time and through earnest experimentation.

Certainly doing a little public journalism here and there will not produce quick answers to newspaper and broadcast declines. Journalists looking to this philosophy for easy fixes for circulation and ratings problems are doomed to frustration. Mystery writer John D. MacDonald had his Travis McGee character declare, "Integrity is not a search for the rewards for integrity. ... It is not supposed to be a productive asset." Likewise, public journalism is not a search for its rewards; it is not supposed to be a productive asset in the term's traditional meaning.

Recovery of both journalism and public life are, however, possible, and as the end of the 20th century approaches, there are reasons for optimism and signs of recovery. The emerging civic renewal movement, changes in corporate processes to empower workers, experimentation in new ways to operate public schools, growing discussion of new ways of organizing living places and communities, increased acceptance of community policing, and the founding of support groups and neighborhood associations are all early and hopeful signs of an awakening of America's civic ethic. *Devolution*, the movement of responsibility away from the federal government to local governments, has resulted in many local governments developing ways to involve citizens in deliberating about choices in areas such as zoning, environmental choices, and even budgetary matters.

Such movement will continue to occur, with or without journalism's recognition and help. It will go much better, however, accomplish more in a shorter time, and advance into more areas of public life if journalists recognize the importance of such movement, validate it as newsworthy (which it most certainly is by any but the most pinched definition) and understand how it coincides with the self-interests of journalists in all their roles—as citizens and practitioners and as partners in an economic venture. Getting to such a point will be a difficult, contentious, and indirect journey, but we must begin.

In order to begin, it is helpful to examine the role of journalism in a modern democracy. Participatory democracy is a function of community. One person alone could not conceive of democracy and, indeed, would have no need of it. However, two or more people with common interests—a community—require democracy if they are to exist in freedom and equity.

Jointly deciding about things, which is the purpose of democracy, is a dynamic that requires three fundamentals:

1. Shared, relevant information;
2. A method or place for deliberation about the application of that information to public affairs;
3. Shared values on which to base decisions about that information.

If any one of these is missing, democratic decision making cannot occur and the democratic community cannot progress. Some call it gridlock.

The last years of the 20th century provide disturbing indications that the necessary shared information and a common place for discussing it are no longer givens. Without those components, values are mere shibboleths that are likely to define and perpetuate differences rather than take advantage of commonalities.

WHAT "INFORMATION" ... ?

Perversely, the component of shared information is endangered by the very pervasiveness of information itself. In the 1990s, we are nearing a state of paralysis caused by the gush of information that technology makes possible. The paralysis arises not in the nature of the information flow itself, for it is neutural, a commodity, even if overwhelming. The paralysis arises out of the culture of society caught in its rush. The crush of information encourages a self-granted immunity from responsibility born of impotence.

Postman (1985), in his ground-breaking *Amusing Ourselves to Death*, addressed the origin of the impotence:

> In both oral and typographic cultures, information derives its importance from the possibilities of action ... But the situation created by telegraphy, and then exacerbated by later technologies, made the relationship between information and action both abstract and remote. For the first time in human history, people were faced with the problem of information glut, which means that simultaneously they were faced with the problem of diminished social and political potency. ... For the first time we were sent information which answered no question we had asked, and which, in any case, did not permit the right of reply. ...

> Thus, to the reverent question posed by Morse—What hath God wrought?—a disturbing answer came back: a neighborhood of strangers and pointless quantity; a world of fragments and discontinuities. (p. 68)

Information overload is spiritually debilitating. In the space of a short newscast or a newspaper front page, one is confronted with five or six matters that seem to equally demand immediate attention, arouse real concern and, in the way they are presented, reinforce one's impotency to affect them.

Faced with such a deluge, the instinct is to withdraw. We are not capable of thoughtfully testing the overwhelming barrage of information bit by bit through discussion or deliberation. We thus reflexively sort out truth or falsity, importance or irrelevance, and caring or not caring through our individual instincts and values; a frantic triage in the overloaded emergency room of the mind.

As if the sheer volume were not daunting enough, when the information constitutes public issues, it arrives at our eyes and ears packaged in hopeless insolubility. It is framed by both politicians and journalists as black-and-white contests, presented through the words of experts and absolutists. Each of the framers has a stake in continuing the argument; none has a stake in resolving it. Average citizens, who do have a stake in resolution, are frustrated by the crush of contextless information and the polarized presentation of issues. The packages seem to have no handles, no place for well-intentioned citizens to begin the search for solutions.

In the mid-1990s, we are seeing only the beginnings of information glut and pervasive polarization. As the tendency grows to give even small matters full ideological weight, our access to information grows almost exponentially. The threatening combination of fundamental bias and endless flow of facts is seen at its worst on the internet, and is dealt with in more detail in chapter 12. For now, simply consider this awful dilemma: If we cannot agree on a body of shared relevance, if the answer to every question must lie at one extreme value or the other rather than in between, public deliberation aimed at deciding things becomes problematic and, in all likelihood, impossible.

... WHAT "AGORA"?

The second requirement of the democratic dynamic is a place or method for deliberation to occur. In ancient Greece, the agora was more than a marketplace. Goods often ranked second in importance to shared information and public deliberation. In Europe and the early United States, the docks and their environs provided an agora of a more informal sort, but nevertheless a place where fresh information was received and the possibilities for its use discussed. When presses became free and commonplace, pamphlets, newspapers, magazines, and books provided a physically dispersed but common, public, and potentially effective agora.

It became theoretically possible for the agora to function at large and without limits. The increasing availability of information, the enhancement of communication, and the mobility provided by mechanical transportation freed human interaction of physical restraints. But something perverse happened: Rather than connecting us, the burgeoning miracles of information, communication, and transportation separated us. In our rush to take advantage of our liberation from the constraints of time and place, we left behind the primary advantage those constraints had dictated: the local community as the center of life; the geographic place where affinity, proximity and tenure made the solution to problems both mandatory and possible.

The retreat into determined isolation may be only beginning. The Information Superhighway of the 21st century, in its rawest form the antithesis of an agora, may further erode the concept of community where democracy is nurtured. That is still an open question. Interconnectivity provides the opportunity for building virtual communities of various sorts, but early experience indicates those nongeographic communities are extremely specialized in their makeup and concerns. The lack of new and effective agoras joins with information overload to render public deliberation aimed at deciding things difficult, if not impossible.

For the present, at least, journalism retains the ability to recognize, maintain, and, if necessary, create agoras where public questions can be discussed and perhaps resolved. Certainly, editorial and op ed pages are a rudimentary form of agora. Some newspapers in the mid-1990s have moved beyond that base, creating a more organized form of deliberation both in their pages and outside, in the community.

The latter causes discomfort among traditionalists, who contend that journalists who create such forums are intruding, abandoning appropriate detachment and creating a conflict by making news while covering it. This comfortable rationalization does not, however, stand honest scrutiny. If a community (or a nation) shows an inability or unwillingness to engage a problem, is it the job of the journalist merely to record that failure? Put another way, is it the ultimate job of the journalist to stand, detached, on a distant mountain and record the end of the world, bearing only the responsibility of getting the time and date correct?

Without active public engagement in issues of the day, which is to say without viable agoras, democracy cannot function properly. Where such discussions and engagements are not occurring, journalists have a responsibility to help it occur.

... AND WHAT VALUES?

Try to engage a roomful of journalists in a discussion about values and their discomfort is palpable; you can see the necks stiffening, hear the teeth grinding in emotional overload.

"We don't deal in values," they grumble. "We tell the news. It's up to the editorial page and the public to worry about values."

They are kidding themselves and the public. Journalism is not now and has never been value-neutral, all protestations to the contrary. Consider what is traditionally "a helluva story"—the senator who steals, the company that dumps chemicals, the farmer who exploits workers. If we, or society, considered those things routinely acceptable, we would not think of them as newsworthy. In reporting them as news, we are acting out of a set of values: Politicians should not steal, companies should not pollute, people should not be exploited.

A large part of our loss of authority with the public, however, stems from that internal contradiction. We claim to be value-neutral, to be simply telling the news, but in doing traditional and widely accepted investigative reporting, we clearly act out of a set of values about honesty, about how the political system should work, and about how companies and people should act.

The fact, to which we are blind but that is obvious to the public, is that we exercise our own values when we choose to and use the convenient claim of value neutrality when citizens want us to expand our reportorial efforts beyond our traditional targets of investigative reporting that we choose and include other areas that they might choose. It comes across to citizens as either judgmental arrogance or a lack of civic concern, creating yet another disconnect between us and the people we are trying to reach and inform.

If we are willing to act out of such beliefs as politicians should not steal, companies should not pollute, and people should not be exploited, what about other, broader but similarly fundamental statements: that this should be a better community; that its problems should be solved; that public life should go well?

If we unflinchingly adopted such values and made them an acknowledged part of our operational culture, many more things than the content of news stories could change. We could, for one, regain some lost standing with the public and, as a result, be more effective in our role in the democratic process.

OBJECTIVES AND OBJECTIONS

How can an increasingly uninvolved and disconnected public maintain the level of public life that is essential to a democracy? At what point in the explosion of raw data can shared relevance be identified and turned to productive use? Who will do that? What will be the origin and form of the crucial agoras where that information is discussed and turned into democratic action? How can the emotionally loaded and personal questions of core values become part of the process, and how can journalists reflect that crucial part?

I believe that most of the answers to these questions can be provided by journalists, but that can occur only if we develop an expanded role, a broader vision of our contribution to public life.

Certainly, present journalistic practices are not suited to the task of providing relevance and the agora. Simply telling the news of a complex society does little to help solve basic problems, for we have spent years carefully detailing them, analyzing them, and raising alarms about them, but still they persist.

Yet many journalists reject the suggestion that there is, or should be, a broader journalistic role than the one we have played. The public, their philosophy declares, must simply take the divinely defined and delivered news and do the best it can. Journalists, they contend, must maintain a pristine distance, a contrived indifference to outcomes, else the news product be contaminated. This is usually, and I believe mistakenly, called objectivity, and the traditional interpretation of it as synonymous with detachment places an impossible burden on journalism.

So pinched a view ignores a practical reality: Our profession's very existence depends on the viability of public life. A public that does not attend to public affairs, that retreats deeply into private life and concerns, has no need of journalists and journalism, for such a public cannot and will not heed either the news or the needs of public life beyond its most immediate surroundings. So journalists have at least as large a stake in viable public life as anyone else. And we have, for now, the ability to affect that viability.

"For now" is an important qualifier. No one can seriously question that journalism in all its manifestations—newspapers, broadcast, periodicals—is in serious trouble with the public. By every measure of circulation, penetration, reach, respect, ratings, revenue generation, and credibility, the vehicles of journalism are, at best, spinning their wheels.

Some journalists argue that the declines are the fault of the audiences; that for the most part everything is fine in the profession—it is those annoying, stubbornly uninterested and increasingly semiliterate people out there who must change. Others argue that the problem is simply that journalism has not caught up with the technological explosion, but most surely will as better technologies are developed. This "it's just over the horizon" attitude assumes, incorrectly, that the journalism of the old technology can effortlessly become the journalism of the new technology by putting on spiffy new clothes.

Still others contend that the gap between journalists and the shrinking consumer pool is simply a matter of discovering the right formula: a magical new, color weather map, just the right mauve-and-off-white news set, a tightly targeted demographic niche. Find that, they say, and a chagrined public will reappear gratefully on your doorstep. All three arguments, although containing bits of truth, trivialize the problems that are inherent in all of the foreboding numerical and behavioral trends that research uncovers about audiences.

Those troubles did not grow out of a string of small, wrong-headed media operational decisions along the way and cannot be reversed merely by making different operational decisions. The loss of attention and authority has arrived on a steadily building tide of discontent bred in Postman's (1985) "neighborhood of strangers and pointless quantity" and fed by an increasingly introverted journalism caught in the same discontent (p. 70). Rather than accurately diagnosing the problem and devising a useful remedy, however, journalists set out in frantic pursuit of the departing audiences. Concerned about our weakening commercial franchise, we ignored our truer and far more valuable franchise: the essential nexus between democracy and journalism, the vital connection with community and our role in promoting useful discourse rather than merely echoing discontent.

The result is that journalism has suffered a fundamental loss of authority; that is, as Rosen (1993) put it, "the right to be heard, the right to be taken seriously, the ability to be persuasive in your account of things" (p. 51). Regaining that authority, that authenticity, must be journalism's first step toward revitalizing itself and public life, but that requires fundamental change, and journalism's deeply embedded culture is resistant to such change.

A WATERSHED DEBATE

Much of that resistance to change is rooted in traditional journalism's determined detachment from the people and events we cover. That detachment, in turn, stems from a peculiar sort of elitism that questions the ability of people to govern themselves; in other words, an elitism that denies the essence of democracy. That such an idea dominates the culture of the only profession to which the Constitution grants total freedom is a particularly cruel and dangerous irony.

It is not an elitism that journalism developed independently; it is a natural outgrowth of the ideas of Democratic realism so forcefully argued in the first decades of this century by Lippmann in "Public Opinion" (1965). His work reflected and supported the idea that a democracy of ordinary people could not possibly function in the post-Industrial Revolution world. His assertions did not go unchallenged. John Dewey, the great democratic philosopher, argued otherwise, and when Lippmann's views eventually prevailed in the debate, the courses of democracy and journalism were set for decades; courses only now being challenged by a restless and cynical populace.

The debate was so fundamental and crucial that it warrants review as we try to understand the ideas of journalistic detachment that dominate the profession's culture and threaten its future.

By the late 1920s, the Industrial Revolution had made it chillingly clear that the placid, manageable democratic practices of an agrarian society were being challenged and changed by what Lippmann (1965) called unseen environments beyond the sight and scope of ordinary people. Never mind that the possibility of nuclear annihilation and the beginnings of the information explosion were still decades ahead: The complex impact of the Industrial Revolution was challenge enough to traditional democratic forms.

Lippmann and Dewey agreed on many things, including the severity of the challenge and most of its causes and symptoms. Where they departed was on the matter of the appropriate response. Lippmann contended that the unseen environment was so vast, entangling, and complex that there was a need to impose some form of expertness between the private citizen and the environment. Social scientists, he argued, should take their place in front of decisions instead of after them. Those disinterested experts should direct their opinions not to average citizens but to a governing elite, shielding what he called the hopelessly inept, bewildered, biased, frivolous, and incurious citizens from the duty and rigor of decision making except for the casting of an occasional vote. That vote would simply be in favor of the "Ins" if things were going relatively well and in favor of the "Outs" if they weren't going well.

Many prophetic things were said by both men during their exchanges, but perhaps the most prescient one came from Dewey. He countered Lippmann's dreary view of the public's potential with a warning: "The very ignorance, bias, frivolity, jealousy, instability which are alleged to incapacitate" ordinary citizens from governing themselves, he wrote, make them even less unable to passively submit to rule by a governing elite (Westbrook 1991, 312).

Lippmann's views, however, prevailed for decades, embodied in the reform movement that swept through governmental and social establishments. Experts would take care of things; citizens merely need stand by and occasionally calculate how happy they were. What happened, however, is that the information developed and possessed by the experts became confused in their minds as superior knowledge and superior knowledge became misunderstood to be wisdom. A huge disconnect developed between the governing elite and ordinary citizens.

Journalism, too, was swept up in the reform movement and its fascination with elitism. Lippmann himself was a journalist and in his bleak way, he concluded that because journalism had to cope with that unseen environment, journalistic efforts were largely wasted on ordinary citizens (1965). Rather, he argued, journalism should serve the specialized class of governing administrators and experts. Journalists and the governing and leadership elites were best suited to debate about and decide what should happen. As insiders, they are far better prepared to know what to do for the rest of us.

One can argue that we are seeing in the 1990s two important and growing reactions against that false construct: the conservative political movement is one; an increasing revitalization of citizen involvement is the other. It is interesting that those two reactions involve the entire political spectrum from conservative to liberal. The conservative revolt is primarily against intrusion by that distanced, specialized government; the largely liberal revolt is an effort to organize people to create their own initiatives around or in spite of government. Whereas one seeks to dismantle, the other seeks to build, but both are essentially grass roots in origin and represent the sound of Dewey's citizens unable to passively submit to the isolated decisions of a governing elite. Both are healthy. Both hold promise if they stay focused on main causes and avoid the pitfalls of runaway ideology.

For journalism, the inevitable consequence of Lippmann prevailing was an almost total, and in most ways calculated, disconnect between journalists and ordinary people. Many national journalists soon saw themselves as part of the elite, which inevitably disconnected them from ordinary citizens. That idea, in turn, seeped into all of journalism, top to bottom. No surprise, then, that a tenet of the conservative movement is antagonism toward what it views as the elitist, liberal media.

That deliberate disconnection, based in elitism and deeply embedded in the culture of journalism, must be overcome, not simply because it offends conservatives (although it surely does), but because it denies the very foundation of democracy.

Lippmann's incisive mind and persuasive writing about the craft of journalism also greatly elevated the profession's standards. He used the idea of objectivity as a philosophical platform for urging new levels of fairness and accuracy. We need to retain that part of his legacy, but the time has come to seriously question our long-standing acceptance of his views of the role of journalists in a democracy and the nature of democracy itself.

The threats of his philosophy to shared information and the agora and the confusion over the application of core values to democratic decision making are too great to ignore. Elitism and the detachment that springs from it are making those threats more severe. Elitism and detachment are cultural traits that journalists can change simply by rethinking them. Other traits are not so easily changed.

❖ T W O ❖

Understanding a Peculiar Culture

The conventions under which journalism operates are rooted in historic and practical circumstance, but unlike medicine or engineering or other professions, they are not governed by immutable rules of biology or physics or other mandates of nature; journalism's conventions are only tangentially governed by the laws of man. This absence of external control means that journalism's culture has evolved into what journalists have chosen it to be. The absence of external imperatives also means that the profession could make different choices.

To understand the choices made and the possibilities that other choices can be made, it is helpful to explore some of the profession's habits of mind and the historic and practical circumstances in which they developed.

BORN IN A DEFENSIVE CROUCH

Congress shall make no law. ...
—First Amendment to the U.S. Constitution

Before there were deadlines, or city editors or county commissioners to catch in some moldy ripoff of taxpayers, there was the First Amendment. The chronology is crucial. It helps account for journalism's fundamental toughness; a congenital, sleeves-rolled-up aggressiveness; a snarly conviction that nice guys don't get newspapers out.

The culture of toughness has more beneath it than the inevitability that many stories, by their nature, are going to make one person or another unhappy, and there is more beneath it than the pervasive maleness of the profession that persists even into the equal-opportunity 1990s. Such realities have helped form the cultural trait of toughness, but they alone cannot explain it. History can. The reality is that the free press was born in a defensive crouch. Its birth certificate was a declaration—significantly, an affirmative negative—that, "Congress shall make no law. ... "

The First Amendment was written to insure that individual Americans' rights were specific and absolute in the face of the establishment of a central government. So long as citizens could gather, talk, write, petition, and be free of an established religion, they could be free to determine how that central government functioned and their lives were led.

It could not have been contemplated, but probably was inevitable, that a large and powerful subculture would grow up around those four words: " ... and of the press." So potent a prohibition as "Congress shall make no law. ... "—consistently buttressed by court decisions—could hardly have resulted in anything else but a subculture of special privilege; the vacuum was too great, the opportunity too unfettered.

As the central government grew more powerful, fought wars, passed laws, instituted taxes, and controlled the economy, the proscription against its incursion on individual freedoms became more meaningful. The growing stakes involved in big government made the arguments about its direction louder and more contentious, the temptations on officialdom's part to mute the criticism grew more appealing, and the journalistic defenses became more fierce.

The First Amendment thus became a glowing crucifix thrust at arm's length against any would-be devil's approach. Aggressive assertion of the right was the prime directive, the source of all else. Don't tread on me? Don't even think about it.

Of course, the amendment does not guarantee that the press be fair, accurate, honest, profitable, or, of course, paid attention to—only that it be free to be none or all of those things, just as can any citizen who picks up pen and paper. Although it was originally written to empower people rather than any institution, it has become, for the organized press, a license to self-define that is unique among U.S. institutions. Neither clergy nor bar nor medicine nor academe can claim, and have validated by the courts, more latitude in action and deed. That enormous latitude is a mixed blessing.

Alexis de Tocqueville (1990) recognized and sardonically reflected on the uniquely free status of America's press early in his writings about his 1832 journey.

> I confess that I do not entertain that firm and complete attachment to the liberty of the press which is wont to be excited by things that are supremely good in their very nature. I approve of it from a consideration more of the evils it prevents than of the advantages it ensures. (p. 184)

Tocqueville also recognized the absolute necessity of that liberty. "In this question ... there is no medium between servitude and license; in order to enjoy the inestimable benefits that the liberty of the press ensures, it is necessary to submit to the inevitable evils that it creates" (p. 185).

Such singular latitude for one group of people can be uncomfortable in a nation of laws. When every other institution's or profession's activities are to some extent limited, journalism is certain to face constant challenge and questioning about its standing to be thus unfettered. Small wonder, then, that the defensive crouch not only remains a part of the culture but virtually defines it.

Although that defensive posture is useful in some ways, and at any rate is historically unavoidable, it makes us dangerously intolerant of outside criticism. We view most serious criticism not as potentially helpful but as a threat to our unfettered status (and we casually dismiss what we consider nonserious criticism.) This low tolerance for outside criticism is based on a fascinating contradiction. Our canon of objectivity declares that the best and most reliable observer in the detached observer, and much of our claim to legitimacy and authority as critics of such institutions as government, is grounded in that outsider status, that noninvolvement. Yet we dismiss many of our critics on the grounds that they are outsiders, laypersons not washed in the waters of our culture, and therefore, knowingly or not, likely to put our crucial independence at risk through the changes they propose. If they really understood our culture and the history and dynamics of journalism, we argue, they could never recommend such changes.

So we try to have it both ways: We insist that our detachment, or noninvolvement, is precisely what legitimizes our criticism, yet we argue that a similar detachment from journalism on the part of our critics invalidates their criticism of us. That contradictory attitude comes very close to defining a priesthood, and it is one of the less endearing attributes that we show to citizens concerned about our influence.

THE TYRANNY OF SPACE AND TIME

How can you think and hit at the same time?
                                                —Yogi Berra, baseball player.

A crowd of reporters is gathered at the foot of Mt. Sinai, awaiting the return of Moses. They spy a figure trudging back towards them, a stone tablet under each arm. They dispatch a runner to meet him. The runner returns, whispers to a TV anchor, who turns to the camera and intones, "Ladies and gentlemen, Moses is returning from the mountain with Ten Commandments from God, the two most important of which are ... "

Journalism's history does not solely account for the way it acts. The craft is both impelled and constricted by its inexorable, self-imposed cycle of publishing or broadcasting: daily, hourly, and, in the world of CNN, instantly. Newspapers do not publish only on days yielding important news. The six o'clock news is at six o'clock whether or not there is news; CNN's top of the hour is the top of every hour, 24 hours a day, 365 days every year.

This relentless periodicity itself begins to define the indefinable: What is news? Senator Joseph McCarthy understood that well; the press conferences used to flaunt his latest list of Commies and fellow travelers were routinely on weekends, most often Sunday afternoons. Even today, one may note how often Sunday morning utterances of pundits and politicians that otherwise would be unremarkable gain false stature in the relative vacuum of Sunday evening newscasts and Monday morning newsholes.

Journalism done well is not easy work. The thousands of individual decisions that go into the reporting, editing, and presentation of a single daily newspaper absorb time and energy as a black hole absorbs light, leaving little time for contemplation. Yogi Berra rejected any notions of contemplation while a fastball was on its way to the plate. Reflex took over. It was a trained reflex, of course, based in innate skill and honed by repetition, but a reflex nevertheless. The physiological complexities of hitting a fast-moving object with a bat—the seeing, the triggering, the muscle reaction—clearly allow no time for thought.

For journalists, the fastball is on its way to the plate every minute and hour and day; usually there is little time to work out complex rationales and delicate balances; simply take a look and swing. Or, as some critics contend, "Ready, fire, aim."

It seems almost perverse, then, that journalism—an important intellectual activity that should involve a careful balance of values, thoughtfulness, judgment, precise word selection, and attention to nuance—must often be performed under severe time and space restrictions. That practicality in itself requires that its practitioners be "powerfully conditioned to its rules and values" (Yankelovich, 1991, p. 250), that they be able to operate on reflex alone.

The tyranny of time and space molds even the basic act of composition. Writing something under severe deadline pressure that will be read in a newspaper or heard on television in a matter of hours or minutes is wholly different from writing done contemplatively and to be read much later and under different circumstances. The difference is not simply of style and structure; it unavoidably becomes one of substance. As Carey (1974) observed:

> [Journalism] is not only literary art; it is industrial art. The inverted
> pyramid, the 5 W's lead, and associated techniques are as much a

> product of industrialization as tin cans. The methods, procedures and canons of journalism were developed not only to satisfy the demands of the profession, but to meet the needs of industry to turn out a mass-produced commodity. [Thus, these canons become] rules of news selection, judgment and writing. ... They are ... determiners of what can be written and in what way.
>
> In this sense, the techniques of journalism define what is considered to be real. ... If something happens that cannot be packaged by the industrial formula, then, in a fundamental sense, it has not happened. (pp. 246–247)

Relying primarily on reflexes—at least, the traditional reflexes—naturally limits the daily journalist's field of view and restricts the possibilities of telling citizens what's really going on beyond the episodic and the fleeting.

The dailiness and hourly-ness of deadlines compels journalists to draw lines of definition and closure, to want to define an outcome simply because the journalist's artificial deadline has arrived. That, combined with the traditional inverted pyramid style of writing, leads to continuing situations being presented as a series of every-24-hour miniclimaxes, a string of episodes each given its own load of artificial significance.

Consider, as an example, coverage of a major trial, such as the O.J. Simpson murder prosecution of 1994 to 1995. In a months-long trial, many days are spent on relative minutia, yet the convention of the inverted pyramid requires that we pick one happening every single day and make it the lead of the story, whether or not it is important in the large picture. General newspapers can mitigate the misleading impact of that convention by giving the story relatively less play on some days than on others; local and network television can choose, in the limited time devoted to news, to simply ignore the story on days when little of importance occurs. In today's world of specialized media, however, there exists both the opportunity and the appetite for endless detail on every meaningful continuing event. Feeding that appetite on the schedule imposed by journalistic periodicity distorts reality and importance. It gives false weight to what the reporter selects as most newsworthy even if, in the larger picture, it is of relatively little importance.

Time and space imperatives also dictate the impermanence of the journalistic product, which not only lowers certain standards but also helps determine content and emphasis. This impermanence helps decide what the writer, and thus the reader, will and will not be concerned about. Daily journalists must write with one eye on the fact that the things being written will surely change in both meaning and importance.

That reality, however, does give periodicity one redeeming, if shaky, virtue: We get to try again tomorrow. Walter Cronkite's rich baritone nightly signature, "And that's the way it is ... " left millions of Americans feeling reassured about the state of their knowledge, but it actually needed a nightly footnote: " ... as far as we know up to this point."

The requirement of periodicity is among the cultural forces that give rise to what Yankelovich (1991) called a "prickly defensiveness" (p. 250) that permeates journalism. When an upset reader or abused news source challenges a reflex that, to the journalist, seems natural and necessary, the conversation often becomes difficult. It did for me, as it has for other editors, when a news source refused to accept what to us is a handy convention. We had reflexively written, "Johnson could not be reached for comment" at our deadline after a few phone calls had failed to raise him. Mr. Johnson, however, considered his response more critical to the story than we had and objected to being portrayed as either out-of-touch or evasive.

"Why didn't you just wait a day to print the story?" It was not a question; it was a demand. My first response was incredulity: Does this guy understand anything? There was some mumbling about deadlines and dailiness and news values and people being able to postpone stories forever by not being available. He wasn't buying it, and he was right. The need to put that story into the newspaper that day without his comment had been driven solely by our compulsion for dailiness. Because we knew something, we were driven to tell other people immediately, even if incompletely and unfairly.

In fact, Weaver and Wilhoit's (1992) studies point out that a majority of journalists, over time, have ranked only two journalistic values (out of 11 asked about, including accuracy) as being "extremely important" (p. 11). Getting information to the public quickly is one of them. Investigating government claims is the other.

Something to Think About

The tyranny of periodicity is real, but at the bottom, it is often only a handy excuse. We manage to meet those looming deadlines because we have trained our reflexes in a certain way; because we view events and the world around us in a certain deeply ingrained way.

What if we were trained in a different way; what if our reflexes, and our worldview, were different? We could still meet those deadlines by exchanging one set of sharp reflexes for an equally sharp set of other reflexes.

DECLARING WINNERS AND LOSERS

"May I have envelopes please ... And the winners are ... "
—Typical show business awards ceremony

The journalistic impulse to define bright lines even in a world of shadows creates another reportorial reflex. Whether after a political debate or a day in court or the passage of legislation, a device thought to engage readers and make the news understandable and personal to them is the sorting out of winners from losers.

Although events other than sports competitions do sometimes make people or institutions clear winners and losers, such final delineations do not occur nearly so often as that defining device appears in newspapers and on the air.

In matters of the democratic process, such as working out a difficult piece of legislation or consent in a neighborhood group, the winners-and-losers approach is a disservice because it ignores the genius and heart of the process. Sorting winners and losers assumes citizens are one-dimensional in their self-interest and encourages them to be so. Even more distressingly, it is a disservice to the core democratic values of consent and compromise. It sends the message that the process of deliberation will inevitably make some people winners and some losers when, in fact, the nature of consent is that trade-offs are made at many levels and wins and losses are rarely clear-cut. The overriding consideration is whether the process of consent has produced something that ultimately will be good for the society and that all can accept, even though it creates some level of disadvantage for one group and some level of advantage for another.

Journalists can help citizens become a public by presenting events from a broader, public point of view, but journalists cannot do that if we do not ourselves see things from a public point of view.

OBJECTIVITY, DETACHMENT AND CREDIBILITY

Worry first about the connections, and the separations you need to make will become clear over time.
—Jay Rosen (1994, March)

As the nation and its newspapers grew and prospered following the Industrial Revolution, philosophical and commercial considerations gave rise to the notion of objectivity as a foundation of U.S. journalism. Some historians attribute its ascendancy to an attempt by art to emulate science: The dominance of scientific thought and methods sanctified the most distanced observer as being the most reliable. Others attribute it to a crasser impulse: the need of publishers in competitive situations to move away from highly politicized, opinion-ated coverage so as to please a broader audience and offend fewer advertisers.

That is an academic argument that will not soon be agreeably settled, but its resolution is not necessary for our purposes. However foggy the reasons for the rise of the notion of objectivity in journalism, its impact on the journalistic culture of today is clear. Objectivity, it is almost universally believed by journalists, is the fount of their credibility.

The perceived need for objectivity created what Rosen (1994) called "separation fever." Journalists have constructed a long list of separations that guide our attitudes, thoughts, and reactions. All are driven by the notion of detachment as an overriding value, a primary virtue. Our operational ethics require that editorial functions are separate from advertising functions; news from opinion; facts from values; reality from rhetoric. The newspaper is separated from other institutions by its duty to report on them, journalists are expected to separate their professional identity from their personal identity, and truth telling is separated from its consequences so that we can tell it like it is. How the journalist feels about something must be separated from how the journalist reports on it. Newsmakers must be separate from those who report the news. In sum, Rosen (1994, March) concluded that, "the journalist's mind is separated from the journalist's soul" (p. 9).

The tradition of detachment declares that these separations are crucial because they underlie our claim to authority: If we maintain the proper separations, then surely our product is pure and will be perceived as such; its objectivity is insured and we therefore will have credibility.

Separation fever runs at various temperatures. Some journalists, in an effort to maintain complete distance from the politics they cover, do not even register or vote. Most newsrooms have policies that range from complete noninvolvement by staffers in any citizen-related activities to less stringent rules that prohibit staffers from engaging in any activity that they or their colleagues might need to write about.

In our effort to get the separations right and persuade ourselves and others that we are properly detached, we engage in endless, arcane hair splittings and rationalizations that strike most citizens not as simply difficult but humanly impossible.

How, citizens properly wonder, can people who profess to not care what happens be trusted to inform us? Why should the public value the perspectives on the importance of events offered by people who insist they have no stake in those events? The journalistic determination to be properly detached also feeds into other cultural traits that have negative ramifications for journalism and public life:

- It not only supports but encourages transience. When caring about a place or circumstance is considered a negative, roots cannot be comfortably put down or useful relationships established; familiarity breeds professional discomfort.
- It insures that certain important things will not be seen as important, or perhaps not seen at all. Determined detachment leads to a kind of blindness about particular things, a trained incapacity to understand part of our environment and the people in it.
- It insures that more will be reported about what is going wrong than what is going right. Reporting on something wrong involves little risk and requires no extension of faith. Reporting on something going right involves the risk that it can always go wrong. Detachment allows us to avoid that risk.
- It deceives us on the question of our credibility with the public. The deeply held belief that detachment insures our credibility creates yet another disconnection with non-journalists, who simply don't see it that way.

Moving away from detachment does not require the professional to abandon journalistic objectivity; they are not the same thing. Consider Dr. Jonas Salk, who discovered a vaccine for polio at a time in the 1940s when it was cruelly crippling thousands of children. He was a professional scientist and as such had to be objective about his data else he would reach wrong conclusions. He also had to be objective because, under the principles of the scientific method, other researchers had to validate his conclusions using the same data.

But he clearly was not detached. He did not wander into the lab and idly speculate if something there might help someone sometime. He went there with an objective—to find a vaccine for polio—and his quest for that goal could not be allowed to impinge on his objectivity. Journalists are in the same situation. We can maintain professional objectivity while not being detached from the implications of what we do. We can care whether public life goes well and yet report accurately and fairly on whether or not it does go well.

Likewise, moving away from detachment does not put our credibility at risk; it reinforces it. Credibility cannot arise from a contrived detachment that sets us apart from other citizens. To the contrary, credibility for journalists, as for any conscientious citizen, arises from other citizens trusting that we and they are broadly aligned in a common cause, that both of us share a desire to improve our lot.

To understand this, picture in your mind someone you know, not a journalist, who has credibility with you and others. That person possesses certain attributes. She or he is probably thought of as intellectually honest, fair-minded, thoughtful, aware of events—you can make your own list. Most importantly, however, you believe that he or she cares about what happens; that you share common concerns about how life goes.

Traditional journalists, who strive for that same credibility, contend that they are intellectually honest, fair-minded, thoughtful, aware of events—that they possess all of those attributes—but insist that they cannot care what happens, or at least must not be caught caring.

The dilemma is that true credibility with others cannot arise from a person, profession, or institution openly professing not to care, not sharing at least some broad common cause with others. People do not value that which they do not trust, and they do not trust (i.e., place credibility in) that which they feel is not useful to them in accomplishing that broad goal of improving their lot in life. The Times-Mirror (1994) survey in which 71% of Americans agreed that "the news media gets in the way of society solving its problems" (p. 160) shows clearly that people do not see journalism as joined in common cause with them.

Something to Think About

Maintaining the proper separations at all costs and against all arguments does not undergird our claim to authority; it undermines it: the detachment that journalists so avidly cultivate is just as avidly distrusted by citizens.

What would happen if journalists spent less time worrying about proper separations and more time worrying about proper connections? Approaching the problem from that angle, we could see the possibilities of appropriate action—ways of doing something—rather than being continuously blinded by the reasons for inaction.

DOES A + Z = BALANCE? ... OR ACCURACY?

... the fact that we begin to know how badly (reporting) is often done, shows that it can be done better.
—Walter Lippmann, "Public Opinion" (1965, p. 166)

The notion of objectivity carries with it a requirement for something called *balance*. The idea is that journalists, being conduits, should carefully offer both sides of virtually any matter under discussion. Every assertion more arguable than that the Earth is round must be matched by a contending assertion. Invoking this axiom supposedly removes any obligation...and risk...on the part of the reporter that people with different views will be offended or left out of the discussion.

Problems with the principle of balance arise, however, in real-world applications.

If a source, for instance, asserts "A," the reporter is obliged to seek balance. This almost always means finding an expert to assert "Z," and reporters with more than passing knowledge of their beats know exactly where to find such a person. He or she is almost always an absolutist on the matter, or else the reporter would not have known to call that particular person.

Seeking "Z" serves two cultural imperatives: It provides the necessary journalistic balance and, important to tradition, it inserts a clear element of conflict into the story. Conflict, real or contrived, is the highest coin in the journalistic realm. Journalists love it and defend their ardor on the grounds that readers also relish it. Clearly, people are drawn to conflict, but where obviously contrived or transparently partisan conflict stands in the way of resolution of important problems, citizen tolerance for it—and those who convey it—becomes strained.

The negative effect of contrived polar conflict is starkly outlined by E.J. Dionne, Jr. in his deservedly best-selling book *Why Americans Hate Politics*. (1992). As he wrote:

> The central argument of this book is that liberalism and conservatism (for their own purposes) are framing political issues as a series of false choices. ... We are suffering from a false polarization in our politics, in which liberals and conservatives keep arguing about the same things when the country wants to move on. (p. 11)

This frustration, he demonstrated, has caused many Americans to give up on the political process because most people are not stuck at either extreme on most issues. They harbor both ambivalence and a desire to get things settled. Framing issues at the extremes defines most people out of the discussion. "If that's what the argument is about," they say, "I'm not in it; my views aren't reflected," so they opt out. The quoted sources (and the journalist who presents them) become participants in a closed, detached cycle.

But there is more to the problem. Where do most of those Americans who hate politics learn about politics? From journalists. The implications of that information-age reality are profound. So long as politicians frame issues at the extremes (and there is no reason to think they will stop) and journalists relentlessly reflect only those false choices, people will be repelled from both politics and journalism.

Seeking balance works perfectly well in those situations where the issue is one-dimensional. Of course, that is not most situations. More often than not, "A" and "Z" provide a falsely simplistic frame, for many of the other 24 letters would provide nuances reflecting the whole array of opinion and possibilities. If the concept of balance is to serve journalism and the public well, it needs to be complete, not polarized.

Our reporting needs to reflect not simply the self-serving false choices portrayed by the antagonists, but the full array of possibilities, the B through Y of the situation. Often, this is simply a matter of framing the story differently.

In 1996, ranchers and environmentalists in Kansas' sprawling Flint Hills faced a difficult issue. The Topeka shiner, a 1-inch subspecies of minnow, lives only in the streams that meander through those vast grasslands. Ranchers wanted to dam some streams for watershed purposes; environmentalists feared that dams would eradicate the Topeka shiner. Several years before, we would have reported that story as a fierce argument between unrelenting opponents, each side intent on having its way, and, indeed, there were such people on each side. The story would have left the reader with a sense of both exclusion and hopelessness, and a less than full understanding of the problem. However, *The Eagle* reporter found a rancher who was also a dedicated environmentalist (as many are) and framed the story through that rancher-environmentalist's conflicting thoughts and emotions.

The rancher-environmentalist's interest was not to prevail at one extreme or the other, as he had no polarized position, but to find a resolution that everyone could accept. The story reflected the arguments of the antagonists, of course, for they were an important part of the situation. The central frame, however, involved the middle ground where resolution could lie, and as a result readers could understand the issue not merely as a bipolar argument but as a public dilemma involving many dramatic elements and subtle considerations. Although not framed at the extremes of the conflict and through the words and eyes of the official combatants, it was hard-hitting, educational, and, of course, had the value of accuracy.

Something to Think About

Every journalistic exploration of an issue cannot, of course, become a full-blown, multifaceted public seminar. But if seeking balance were viewed not as an exercise in journalistic technique but as an opportunity to include more people in the cycle, wouldn't we go about seeking balance somewhat differently, and with more care?

THE ADVERSARY AXIOM

If your mother says she loves you, check it out.
—Journalism professor John Bremner

The other value that Weaver and Wilhoit (1992) found that a majority of journalists consider "extremely important" is "investigating government claims" (p. 11). Historic origins help explain that relationship.

The purpose of the First Amendment's hands-off admonition to government was to insure that criticism of authority could not be foreclosed.

In today's world, whether or not government or journalism is comfortable with the idea, the watchdog role implicit in the First Amendment locks government and journalism into a symbiotic relationship. Neither can get along without the other; neither can survive if the other becomes dominant. Such a healthy symbiosis between government and journalism is essential and life-sustaining not only for the partners but for a third entity—democracy.

Our aim as journalists should be to insure that Americans understand the true choices they have about issues so they can see themselves, their hopes, and their values reflected in the democratic process. Because the relationship is symbiotic, we cannot accomplish that aim if either partner abandons or poisons the relationship.

The watchdog role that inexorably springs from the First Amendment has served journalism (and democracy) well in dealing with government. Journalists routinely and casually refer to their relationship with government as adversarial, and contend that it is naturally and properly so. But, as Lambeth (1986) pointed out:

> There is a real sense in which an uncritical embrace [of the adversarial posture] forecloses the critical thinking needed in moral reasoning. There is a sense in which an adversarial posture becomes an ideology that prevents the sensitive interpretation and application of the principles of humaneness, truth telling, justice, freedom/independence, and the stewardship of free expression. (p. 99)

Instead, Lambeth (1986) argued, skepticism is the useful posture; adversarialism, with its many limiting factors, can sometimes, and unavoidably, result from healthy skepticism, but the relationship should not begin there.

Unfortunately, journalism's determined adversarial relationship with government is not confined to that; it reaches into and damages our relationship with all authority, and even beyond to our dealings with regular citizens. This has proven to be less than helpful. The downside of the fists-up, gnarly attitude that we have cultivated in dealing with officialdom is clear when a journalist identifies himself or herself on the phone to an average citizen unaccustomed to dealing with us. You can hear the hesitation at the other end, almost feel the concern: Uh oh, this can't be anything good. Yet the late Kansas University journalism professor John Bremner's oft-quoted admonition, "If your mother says she loves you, check it out," is an important one. There are many good reasons for being wary and checking it out, not all of them cynical. For instance, somebody may simply be mistaken. When a relentless adversarial attitude becomes an end in itself, however, useful communication is threatened and often foreclosed. This has important ramifications, many of them negative, for journalists, their sources, and their audiences.

As with any relationship, balance is the key. For years, the Knight–Ridder Washington Bureau was graced by a framed photograph of its legendary first bureau chief, Ed Lahey, an ex-Chicago tough-guy reporter. Of the many pithy quotes Lahey employed to educate his troops, the one memorialized under the photo was perhaps the most telling: "Fawn Not Upon The Mighty."

That is a useful admonition in the heady atmosphere of the nation's capital and reflects the proper skeptical attitude between reporters and the large and powerful figures on which they report. However, the deliberate distancing can also lead to frustrations and misunderstandings both large and small, serious and comic.

Vice-President Lyndon Johnson, on a campaign swing through the Carolinas, was much taken by a story in the *Charlotte Observer*. He called the newsroom unannounced, as he was wont to do in those days, and asked for the reporter, Dwayne Walls. He was told abruptly, "He's gone home," … click. LBJ called back and "Gus" Travis, a former columnist finishing out his career on the desk, answered once more. "This is Lyndon Baines Johnson, Vice-President of the United States," Johnson announced, "and I'd like to speak to Mr. Dwayne Walls." "Well, this is Augustus Zollicofer Travis, copy editor and headline writer, and he's not here," Travis snapped.

Something to Think About

A healthy skepticism about government, authority of any kind, and the unsubstantiated claims of citizens is vital to what we do. An unrelenting, all-purpose adversarialism stands in the way of things we should do. Do we think enough about the difference? And what could happen if we did?

IS THAT ALL THERE CAN BE?

This is not an argument against such useful cultural traits as proper separations or an appropriate skepticism-driven position in relation to government. It is not a plea for that most dreaded of journalistic conditions, softness. Journalism's birth in a defensive crouch is unavoidable—and useful—history. I do, however, suggest that when proper separations mutate into unconcerned detachment and determined toughness becomes a singular aim and attribute, things go fundamentally wrong for both journalism and public life. Fixing them will require rethinking journalism's culture and the how and why of its development. It will require opening our minds to additional elements in the definition of *good journalism*.

Because journalism operates with no external proscriptions or rules for participation or other legal requirements, excesses are not only possible but inevitable. To fend against the threats to the First Amendment that such excesses spawn, the mainstream journalism community has, over time, developed certain conventions, generally agreed-on ways of operating. Although these mores are self-generated and adherence to them is voluntary, they take on the patina of membership requirements, sometimes even of canons. Those who subscribe to them believe that good journalism is that which adheres to the generally accepted mores, and anything else is less than good journalism.

From time to time, and usually in response to the public's concerns about excesses, various groups in the mainstream profession have attempted to codify those mores. However, such efforts at establishing codes of ethics or canons of behavior have always fallen short of universal acceptance because of the fiercely independent bent of the people who are attracted to journalism.

One result of journalism's self-conscious defensiveness about its great latitude is that mainstream journalism is reluctant to question and slow to change those mores that, through general acceptance and long use, approach the status of canons. Yet the practices that underlie those canons constantly change.

Fifty years ago, presidents were not quoted directly unless they made a formal speech; the conventions of White House coverage absolutely forbade it. Even 35 years ago, circumspection had its place. In the midst of the Vietnam war, President Lyndon Johnson sought to force North Vietnam to the peace table with a bomb-and-talk strategy. A visiting group from Charlotte, where I was city editor at the *Observer*, met with him in the Rose Garden on a steamy July afternoon. Clearly weary and troubled, the president lapsed into eerie monologue.

He had been up almost all night conferring with his military people in Washington and Saigon, he said, and he was frustrated. "I bombed 'em last week and nothing happened. So I hit 'em again last night," he said. The stunning personalization by the most powerful man in the world never got into print. Editors at the *Observer* felt that it was off-limits despite the absence of acknowledged ground rules and the fact that some 90 citizens of Charlotte heard it. Today, properly, every presidential word, nuance, and slip is fair game, not simply to pass along but to analyze, comment on, and archive for later use.

Forty years ago, news stories routinely referred to the race of the people involved—if they were other than White, of course. It was, in the eyes of many, a convention to help a predominantly White audience sort out perceived importance. In most news operations today, racial references appear only where they are directly pertinent to the circumstances.

Thirty years ago, routine stories always included an address of the person involved; it was basic, required by convention. A rookie reporter who came back without a specific address risked at least a stern lecture. In today's privacy-conscious atmosphere, stories include specific addresses only when unusual circumstances require it.

In each case, reasons emerged that most journalists considered sufficient to warrant change. Again, the purpose here is not to debate the merits of those changes but to demonstrate that today's rules may not be tomorrow's; that journalism, like any other institution, finds reasons to change even the small things. Because of the defensive crouch in which we operate, however, virtually all of those changes are self-generated and come only over time. We now examine (chapters 3 through 7) how that process of gradual change operated on one journalist and address some questions of whether it needs to be that way.

Something to Think About

David Mathews (1993) of The Kettering Foundation and Daniel Yankelovich (1991) address the issue of journalistic mores in slightly different, but insightful, ways. Interestingly, both characterizations reflect faint echoes of a priesthood.

Yankelovich: " ... The media are dominated by a powerful subculture that repels outsiders and powerfully conditions insiders to its rules and values. In recent years, the media have grown increasingly conscious of their vast influence; they take pride in it but do not know quite what to do with it. They are more comfortable when criticizing others than when being criticized, and they tend to be thin-skinned, prickly, and defensive." (p. 14)

Mathews: "It is important to differentiate between the canons of the profession and the axioms of professionalism that have grown out of them. Objectivity, for instance, [shouldn't disappear] but some silly axioms about it, such as not caring [should]." (p. 15)

PART II

❖ T H R E E ❖

Learning to Not See

In 1958, the newsroom of the *Charlotte Observer* was the center of the universe for 100 or so journalists in various stages of transition. Some, the older ones, were outward bound, winding down careers at The Gray Lady of South Tryon Street, as the paper was called by its progressive detractors. Others, the younger ones, were upward bound, starting careers at a newly rejuvenating newspaper purchased in 1954 by John and Jack Knight and presided over by the mannerly although kinetic C.A. (Pete) McKnight.

The flavor of change permeated the cluttered, functional 3 story building 6 blocks south of "The Crossroads of the Carolinas," the intersection of Tryon and Trade streets. These two streets formed Independence Square—although there wasn't a proper square—and were the commercial heart of a city of 275,000 teetering on the ridge between The Old South and The New South. It was Pete McKnight's charge, from the Knights and their brilliant editorial guru, Lee Hills, to make sure that it was not the magnolias that prevailed.

Transforming The Gray Lady to meet the challenges of the second half of the 20th century would take energy, talent, and nerve. The comfortable city ruled by a White male, traditionalist leadership was accustomed to an equally comfortable relationship with its two newspapers, the morning *Observer* and the afternoon *Charlotte News*. Each had been owned by local families until the Knights arrived from Akron, Ohio with their big dollars and bigger ambitions and picked off the *Observer*, and, a few years later, the *News*. In 1959, the two newspapers and the Associated Press' Carolinas operation were all jammed into the South Tryon building.

McKnight, with a shrewd eye for talent, persuaded Tom Fesperman, managing editor of the *Charlotte News*, to move to the *Observer* in 1956. Fesperman's insight on talent was equally sharp, having been honed in the underdog atmosphere of the smaller *News*. Together they lured an astonishing parade of promising graduates and near beginners to the *Observer*, plus one young sports writer from the University of North Carolina at Chapel Hill.

I arrived at the paper in 1958 after spending a year as a sports correspondent for the newspaper while at Chapel Hill. The job of covering the Atlantic Coast Conference was a handoff from Jack Claiborne, who had joined the Observer's sports department after graduating from UNC in 1957. Libby and I, high school and college steadies since 1953, married the day after my graduation and began a journey that was to take us to six cities in five states; provide the world with a doctor, a media relations expert, and a nurse; and pass through wrenching change in our society and profession.

In Charlotte, as the 1950s turned into the 1960s, Claiborne and I watched as the McKnight—Fesperman tandem transformed the staff. In his 1986 history of the *Observer*, Claiborne calculated that more than a dozen of the recruits in those years became editors or publishers of newspapers. Among the editors, Larry Jinks (*Miami Herald, San Jose Mercury-News*) also worked for a time as a Knight–Ridder vice-president for news, and James K. Batten, recruited by McKnight from nearby Davidson College, was once editor of the *Observer* itself and later the parent corporation's chairman and CEO. Rolfe Neill, now the *Observer* publisher, presided over the *Philadelphia Daily News* and the *New York Daily News* before returning to Charlotte. Papers in Providence, Rhode Island; Dallas; Winston–Salem, North Carolina; Fayetteville, North Carolina; Anderson, South Carolina; Akron, Ohio; Portland, Oregon; Charleston, South Carolina; Bradenton, Florida; and, of course, Wichita were also among those headed by McKnight–Fesperman hires from that period.

In addition, scores of bright reporters, copy editors, and photographers learned there and moved to other newspapers and magazines, large and small, around the country. In short, if there was a journalistic virus at the *Observer* in those years, it was bound to spread to many other newspapers. There was, indeed, a virus.

A visitor to the *Observer* newsroom in 1960 would not have noticed any immediate differences other than age between the young recruits and the veterans. Shirts (white, like all the faces) and ties for the men and business dress for the small number of women, all of whom were limited to writing of pastry and parties for the women's pages. But the twentysomethings differed from their elders in a major way. Born just before World War II and raised in the relative peace and prosperity of the postwar boom, we were graduating from liberal arts and journalism programs at places like UNC Chapel Hill, Columbia University, Michigan, and Missouri with substantial questions about the society we inherited and the beginnings of doubt about our parents' definition of postwar success: steady job, suburban house, station wagon, cookouts, and Scrabble on Saturday nights.

The bucolic upbringings, the optimism about ever-more-successful careers and the orderly view of things was already haunted by fears of nuclear disaster and challenged by a host of intellectual notions emerging from Moscow to Montgomery and back. In our first full decade of work as journalists we would watch and report on:

- American political violence of an unprecedented nature, with the murders of John F. Kennedy, Robert Kennedy, Martin Luther King, Jr., Malcolm X, and Medgar Evers; the gunning down of protesting students at Kent State University; and Chicago police tear gassing and beating hundreds of protesters at a national political convention. We would see, live on television, Jack Ruby cut down Lee Harvey Oswald.
- Blacks, trying to attend public schools, spat on and attacked by police dogs, and Governor George Wallace standing in the doorway of the University of Alabama. We would argue about the theory of interposition and laws against miscegenation, and debate about the difference between integration and segregation.
- Hundreds of thousands of our peers going off to Vietnam, 57,000 of whom would die trying to stop the spread of communism, as thousands more took to the streets to try to stop the spread of the war.
- The surreal sight of a man walking on the surface of the moon, although U.S. technological expertise was unable to produce an inexpensive automobile that worked better than imports and our national will was unable to produce responses to the rising tide of ignorance and poverty in the exploding inner cities.
- The United States and the Soviet Union sailing toward the brink of nuclear war over Cuba.

The thunderous events of that decade fueled our confusion over our journalistic roles. It was not a time for dampened passions or for cool objectivity, yet our journalistic training and the traditional culture of our craft required precisely that.

THE UNCOMFORTABLE ARMOR OF DETACHMENT

In self-defense, most of us tried on the armor of detachment. It was our job, there in the center of the universe at 600 South Tryon Street, to collect, write, copy edit, caption, and headline the words and pictures of a maelstrom of change unequalled in so brief a period of the nation's history. It was our assignment to process and ship out to the far corners of the Carolinas a product—news—with its own reason

for being, needing no justification other than it was something that was
known and therefore of some level of importance. What people did
with it, how it affected them (or even whether they cared) was not a
question we were supposed to worry about. At least, that's what the
inherited culture dictated.

We did, of course, care a great deal about what was happening; the
armor of detachment pinched in critical places and had gaping holes
in others. Although we doggedly rationalized professional detachment
into a virtue, we could not stand coolly by while our world was aflame
with protest and discontent and threatened by holocaust, both nuclear
and social. It was our future that was threatened. Claiborne (1986)
reflected on those years:

> The ten years ... were among the most contentious in American history,
> and in that time the *Observer* all but exhausted its store of reader good
> will. In standing again and again for what it thought was wise and just,
> even when it proved unpopular, the paper got ahead of its audience and
> nearly crossed the line between community conscience and arrogant
> scold. As a result, the paper itself was often an object of controversy. (p.
> 251)

We were the hardened shock troops of what we saw (like every
previous generation) as a bright new age of journalism. Because of our
times, however, we were caught in the contradiction of caring deeply
about some things but being professionally admonished that we could
not, under the Rule of Objectivity, concern ourselves with consequences so long as we published accurate information. Whether any
of the news had meaning beyond the context of our journalistic
processing was officially the business of the editorial writers, not of
the people in the newsroom. For some, the contradictions between
task and reality became overwhelming.

I recall overhearing a young reporter loudly berating a school
bureaucrat about "commie propaganda" in a textbook and accusing
her of subverting young minds with "thinking right out of the Kremlin."
The reporter soon left the staff and wound up writing speeches for
Barry Goldwater's presidential campaign. And a proofreader going
over the edge and changing every reference in a school-desegregation
story from Negro (the then-preferred racial designation) to "nigger," as
in, "Jones, also a nigger." The story appeared in the first edition before
it was caught and the offender fired. And a copy editor who could not
write one more headline about the fall of yet another Vietnamese village
and the official body count pronouncement simply putting down his
pencil and walking out. And a weeping reporter awakening an assistant
city editor at 5 a.m. to say, "They have killed Bobby Kennedy" and
getting in his car to drive to California just to be there.

For others, salvation lay in finding ways around the tough nut of detachment versus humanity. Sometimes the shock troops became snipers, lurking in the bushes to strike some blow, no matter how small, for those things that we in fact cared deeply about.

The county commissioner's nickname was "Hub." A cotton farmer from the rural part of the county, he had been consistently reelected on the basis of a good ol' boy image projected with a syrupy Southern accent and protected by the backing of an old-line, downtown Democratic Party hierarchy comfortable with its control of him. He was, to them, safe. But Hub, true to his origins, was a redneck, physically and spiritually, something all the courthouse reporters knew but had not the journalistic arsenal to report, for he was as cautious in public as he was outrageously virulent in private. So we waited in the bushes.

One of the county board of commissioners' dreary but necessary duties was to hear appeals by potential welfare clients who had been denied aid because of some technical ineligibility under the complex and often conflicting rules of Washington and Raleigh. The board had limited authority to make exceptions, and often did so.

Heading the Welfare Department was Wallace Kuralt, a kind-hearted, deeply intellectual man who sometimes bore dyspeptically the burdens of his office. (He was the father of now-retired CBS correspondent Charles Kuralt, who reported for several years in the 1950s at the *Charlotte News*, a precursor of the McKnight–Fesperman cadre.) At the end of a long county board session, Wallace Kuralt was presenting the case of a White family who had fallen between the regulatory cracks. As the forlorn woman and her three grimy kids stood by, the commissioners heard Kuralt's plea and voted no, 4 to 1, a visibly angry Hub dissenting. "There's something I jes cain't understand," he blurted after the vote. "Why is it that we can help all these niggers that Wally brings up here and we cain't help this poor White family?"

Bang! Clean head shot. I cared very much about reporting that, and did so, faithfully recreating the "nigger" vernacular. Hub's phone starting ringing at 6 a.m., and later that day, fuming, he jumped me in the courthouse:

"Why'dya put that in the paper?" he demanded.

"Well, Hub, that's what you said."

"Naw, I didn't. I said KNEE-gra," drawing out both full, fat syllables.

"Hub, I'm sorry, but I have never heard you say 'KNEE-gra' until this very minute. We can go listen to the tape and you tell me how to spell it."

It was his last term. His telling outburst made him a liability to the downtown power elite. The journalistic execution of Commissioner Hub qualified as just telling the news, of course, because he was pilloried by his own public words. In my private view—then, as now—a greater good was accomplished; a moral imperative was upheld.

For me now, the story of Commissioner Hub is interesting because it illustrates how a morally charged environment can change the application of the rules, tolerating the development and use of techniques that might be considered inappropriate in lesser circumstances.

Something to Think About

What constitutes a changed environment in which extraordinary techniques are appropriate? It is not a question journalists like to think about, in part because of the deeply embedded tradition of detachment that holds us as somehow immune from our environment, and in part because telling the news is demanding enough work on its own. But do not the declines in public life and in journalism constitute a troubling moral environment that warrants extraordinary techniques?

THE CHANGE OF NOVEMBER 1963

The newspaper journalists of the 1960s would face another challenge: They would see with stunning clarity that they were no longer alone in the business of telling news. With the assassination of John F. Kennedy, the televising of political conventions, and the engrossing live pictures from the surface of the moon, journalism changed from a craft of after-the-fact reportage to a craft of real-time coverage. The pace and direction of that change would have a lasting effect, for good or ill, on the profession and the American people.

The era of high-impact, live television news arguably began at 1:45:45 p.m. EST on Friday, November 22, 1963, when NBC News broadcast a bulletin nationwide:

> President Kennedy and Governor John Connally of Texas were cut down by an assassin's bullet in downtown Dallas and were rushed to an emergency room at Parkland Hospital. The President's limp body was seen cradled in the arms of his wife. There is no information at present on his condition. (National Broadcasting Company, 1966, p. 1)

For the next 5 days, Americans would be riveted to television sets as never before. All three major networks went to saturation coverage, creating an unprecedented audience mass. Although an alleged shooter was in custody within hours of the assassination, the context of the Cold War, tensions with Cuba, and turmoil in the United States over civil rights created a climate in which almost any scenario was imaginable.

Although the array of conspiratorial alarms was broad, the network anchors did not deal in the currency of speculation that day; they sought no unknown, immediate answers; spun no instant analysis. The stakes were too high, the journalistic traditions too strong. And, of course, the technology was limiting. At one point in the grainy, black-and-white kinescopes of the day, one can see a network announcer holding a telephone up to a desk microphone in a gray-walled studio, struggling to get the voice of a reporter in Dallas out to the nation.

Without instant hookups to every square mile of the globe, Americans were denied a certain level of basic information in those early hours, but they also were spared reckless speculations from uninformed sources and hastily assembled panels of experts constructing theories and spinning scenarios on insufficient facts. Neither was there any attempt to put the horrendous event instantly into perspective. When a weary David Brinkley signed NBC off at 12:51 Saturday morning after the Friday assassination, he said simply:

> We are about to wind up, as about all that could happen, has happened. It is one of the ugliest days in American history. There is seldom any time to think any more, and today there was none. In about four hours we had gone from President Kennedy in Dallas, alive, to back in Washington, dead, and a new president in his place. There is really no more to say except that what has happened has just been too much, too ugly and too fast. (National Broadcasting Company, 1966, p. 46)

Even if the events of that Friday had been too much, "about all that could happen" had not yet happened. On Sunday, November 25, at 12:20 p.m., Lee Harvey Oswald, accused of the assassination, was being escorted through the basement garage of the Dallas City Jail for transfer to the more secure county jail. A pistol was thrust out of a mass of people, including NBC cameramen and reporters; there were popping sounds; a white-Stetsoned deputy recoiled, surprise distorting his face; Lee Harvey Oswald's handcuffed arms crossed at his chest, his mouth formed a wounded "o." The figure holding the gun, dark suit, dark felt fedora, seemed more suited to a 1937 gangster film than to 1963.

Despite Jack Ruby's throwback attire, millions of Americans were plunged at that instant into a new age of communication, awareness, and intellectual challenge. Brutal and shocking though it was, they had witnessed a major and unexpected event in U.S. history as it unfolded.

For many, the murder of Lee Harvey Oswald was anticlimactic, for some even a compensatory relief, compared with Kennedy's death 2 days before. They had not, however, witnessed the President's assassination; there was only one grainy, amateur movie strip of the horror of Dealy Plaza, and it was not available for broadcast until more than a week later. Live murder was palpably different, its impact immediate and without the padding of even a few minutes to absorb the shock.

Again, the networks were restrained. Because of the enormous popularity of Chet Huntley and David Brinkley, NBC drew more viewers than ABC and CBS combined and decided to stay on the air continuously from 6:59 a.m. Sunday until after the Monday funeral. (The actual sign-off wound up being at 1:18 a.m. on Tuesday.) During that time, the funeral plans were made and announced, Kennedy's body lay in state in the Capitol rotunda, foreign dignitaries began arriving in Washington, Lee Harvey Oswald was to be transferred to the more secure jail, and a new president was in the first challenging days of painful transition.

At the time of the funeral itself, on Monday afternoon, 95% of the American people were watching television. Historian William Manchester (1967) observed that such a 42-hour broadcast with all of the events spinning around it:

> In irresponsible hands, could have been dangerous. The possibilities were Orwellian. ... Brinkley later calculated that "the shocked and stunned nation was listening to six people at most, us commentators. It would have been so easy to start a phony rumor that would never die, that would be alive fifty years later." Fortunately, the half-dozen broadcasters took their responsibilities seriously. ... Each man tried to avoid exciting, provoking or irritating his listeners. ... [D]uring the rotunda ceremonies or the funeral ... they let events unfold for themselves. Sometimes as long as fifteen minutes would pass with no comment whatsoever. (p. 530)

It was, by today's reckoning, dull television: unbroken quarter hours of funereal music as thousands edged silently past the closed casket; hushed commentary; few repeats of the sensational scene from the basement of the Dallas City Jail; even fewer speculations and alarums. Despite the restraint and responsibility of the network coverage in that winter of 1963, everything about journalism had changed. Newspapers could never again be first with breaking news. As television began developing its own standards for daily spot news, newspaper journalism began a tortured, 30-year search for its place in a revolutionized environment.

Something to Think About

The first response of newspapers to live television news was to differentiate by putting emphasis on depth, background, detail and analysis—things that television could not do. That was not sufficient to overcome TV's power of shallowing appeal, so newspapers began to be more like TV in approach and content. Not surprisingly, that has not worked.

Meanwhile, television has attempted to become more like magazines. In each case, imitation was the sincerest form of missing the point, for each move involved conceiving of people as consumers to be won in a mortal competition, rather than as a public capable of action.

MORE AND MORE NEWS

Those young journalists of the 1960s pursued their careers into the 1970s and 1980s propelled by events that were themselves propelled—and sometimes created—by exploding technology. The profession we had chosen was, suddenly, not the profession we had inherited. Change, so welcome and easy a companion at the beginning of the decade, was now a pestering, nattering scold, rushing ahead of our capacity, yelling back for us to catch up.

We still considered ourselves to be in the business of telling the news, but, suddenly, there was so much more news to give; that is to say we had more and more immediate access to more and more information. We, and television, were propelled into a frantic triage mode. We developed the capacity, the staffs, the machines, and the mission of processing more and more data. We sent it out, the processed and delivered factual record—constant and growing amounts of information, sometimes with immediate context added, sometimes without. A glut of data, sometimes important only because we knew about it and the amorphous *they* didn't, and therefore it had to be told.

By feeding the flood, we were beginning to create Postman's (1985) "world of fragments and discontinuities," sending out endless information "which answered no question [anyone] had asked and ... did not permit the right of reply" (p. 68).

We carried out our worthy, perhaps ennobling occupation safe in the womb of "The Great Concrete Momma" as Dan Lynch of the *Albany Times Union* tellingly labeled newspaper buildings. Comfortingly, our culture not only allowed but required our detachment from the rest of the world, that our truth telling be separated from its consequences; that our personal identity be separated from our professional; that we be properly distanced from the people we reported on.

Journalistic routines, however, inevitably become ways of seeing the world that are particular to journalists. And, as Rosen pointed out, they therefore become ways of not seeing, a trained incapacity to recognize certain realities (personal communication, 1993). The journalistic sense of priorities and view of the world is not only strongly shaped by the mechanical conventions and peculiar culture of news gathering, it is also limited by them.

Something to Think About

Because we were totally absorbed in sending information out and were barred by detachment from allowing anything important back into the newsroom center of our universe, we were missing something crucial about the needs and realities of public life.

❖ F O U R ❖

Soaring Toward a Crash

It was not apparent to journalists soaring into the 1970s that we were missing something crucial. Neither journalism nor the business side of the media, those often uneasy partners that together provide the news in newspapers and on television, saw many clouds on the horizon.

The domestic trauma of the 1960s had eased somewhat with the passage of Lyndon Johnson's civil rights package, and the political killings had stopped, at least at home. The political carnage in Vietnam continued, as did the protests in America, but public school desegregation was under way surely, if not smoothly. Richard Nixon was promising an economy that would be good for business, and business was responding. For the twentysomethings of the 1960s, the 1970s were a time of cooler passions, for getting on with life as thirtysomethings.

For the business side of journalism, the landscape was also changing, particularly for newspapers. Inheritance tax laws, favorable capital gains tax treatment, and the constant growth imperatives of Wall Street virtually mandated an era of aggressive acquisition by newspaper companies. Knight Newspapers and Ridder Publications were snapping up single-owner newspapers and talking about a potential merger that would make the combined company the nation's largest in terms of circulation. Gannett was on the prowl, *USA Today* not yet a gleam in Al Neuharth's eye. Bidding for available newspapers in monopoly markets was vigorous. In 1900, only 27 dailies were owned by groups. In 1960, the number was 560. And in the 1980s, it would rise to well over 1,000.

Television's driving force—audience ratings—continued to soar on its impetus from the 1960s. It would be 1977 before any sign of leveling could be noted; certainly in 1970 no one could see an end to the spectacular growth. The three major networks dominated, the specter of cable-driven competition still down the road.

For journalists and would-be journalists, the corporate explosions meant greatly expanded opportunities. In the decade between 1971 and 1981, jobs in journalism increased by an astonishing 61% (Weaver

44

& Wilhoit, 1992). The movement of control to corporate headquarters, however, quickly began to pose serious questions about journalistic mission, both journalists' personal missions and those of the giant holding companies. The pressure for ever-fatter bottom lines that springs from the growth imperatives of public ownership (but ignores the reality that newspapers are fundamentally cyclical businesses) was troubling for those who, realistically or not, viewed journalism first as a calling and only peripherally as a business.

My first encounter with this new and uninviting reality had come at the *Observer* in early 1968 with Editor Pete McKnight's stunning declaration that henceforth the newsroom would actually have to live within its budget! It was a notion from some commercial netherworld. What did money have to do with telling the news? If there is no money but lots of news, will we simply not tell the news? How could this be?

Not to worry, we were told: The Knights were preparing to take the company public, a move that would mean great things to all of us. But, meanwhile, Wall Street and the Securities and Exchange Commission have this fixation on numbers and fiscal controls, so learn how to operate within the budget. Everybody is doing it.

And indeed they were. The exponential expansion of public newspaper company holdings extracted its price. One view, that of James Squires (1993) in his book *Read All About It!* is that the price was the ruination of good newspapering. The dirty little secret about corporate ownership, he contended, is that it is incompatible with the good journalism that was so broadly practiced before creeping corporatism took over.

My view of the effect of corporatism is both less sanguine and less nostalgic. Through 24 years as an editor, I have written more than my share—at least in the eyes of several Knight–Ridder (K–R) corporate targets—of memos railing against what I saw as unfair and unreasonable fiscal restraints on our journalistic efforts. In 1978, Larry Jinks, then vice-president for news at Knight–Ridder, felt compelled to distract me from my editing duties in Wichita to fly overnight to Miami for a little chat about my monthly newsroom report, distributed to all K–R editors, that referred to "the dismantling of the newsroom" because of budget restraints. It was an uncomfortable 2-hour session, and expensive, given the cost of no-advance airfare from Wichita to Miami. On my return, in a desperate attempt to reinforce our dire budgetary straits, I sent him the bill for the flight. ("Your meeting," I figured.) He rejected it. ("Your error," he figured.)

Journalism's fiscal piece of the media pie is indeed smaller, and for reasons that have more to do with avarice than is comforting. The problem for publicly held newspaper companies lies in the tyranny of historically high operating returns. Whereas most industries' operating returns may be a few percentage points, newspapers, in their prepublic days, could return 40% or more simply by opening the doors. A tradition of low wages helped build that level of return.

Once those moneymakers are acquired by publicly held companies, the stock market insists that returns increase, or, at the very least, remain steady, year after year. When revenues are not increasing, as is the general case today, the return must be maintained or increased by reducing costs. When that pinch reaches a certain level, quality is sacrificed.

If there were a realistic present alternative to corporate ownership driven by Wall Street, it might be alluring. There is not. The sharks of Wall Street know a good meal when they see one, and 20% to 40% returns are always a good meal. If the managers and officers of media companies were suddenly seized by fervor for better journalism at the expense of bottom lines, they would not for long be the managers and officers.

There is no intrinsic reason why newspaper companies could not operate on a much smaller margin, even single digits, particularly when technology is reducing basic production costs and the entry fee, but today's newspaper companies remain forever captives of their affluent, and often penurious, history. It is impossible, in the present environment of Wall Street, to get from historic 20-plus margins to new single-digit ones without a collapse in the stock price, which would automatically lead to a change in management or an unfortunate takeover. That is because mutual fund managers and the great majority of individual investors are interested in financial return, period. It is of no consequence to them whether or not newspaper companies invest in better journalism; they can always find another investment or somebody else to run the existing one the way they want it run.

As more and more newspapers have been acquired by public companies, operating those companies has become a delicate balancing act between civic responsibility and hard fiscal realities.

Something to Think About

Railing against those realities and the judgments of history is nonproductive activity. Nostalgic yearnings for a return to the good old days of hefty staffs and virtually unlimited budgets is not only nonproductive, such a return would not solve the problems that journalism faces in the 1990s. As we shall see, having more and more people to tell more and more news would not, in itself, solve the dilemma in which we find ourselves. The virtually unlimited newsroom budgets of the 1960s and 1970s would not automatically translate into better journalism in the 1990s. Some other, non-resource-based things must change first.

THE DANGERS OF TRANSIENCE

The explosion of corporate ownership changed a part of the journalistic equation more crucial than the bookkeeping. It turned journalists into careerist transients.

Historically, journalists have had a bit of gypsy in them, harking back to the time when printers with a shirttail full of type migrated across an expanding continent looking for new opportunity. However, the growth of chain ownership and the expansion of television news in the middle part of this century birthed new battalions of journalistic shock troopers anxious to make their careers with little concern for how their work affected life in one place because they would soon be in another. Transience reinforces detachment; detachment encourages transience.

The new mobility driven by corporate expansion simply mirrored the restiveness of all businesses and society at large, but increased mobility for journalists had a more pronounced effect than does mobility in most other professions. A transferred department store manager might take away a family and leave behind some acquaintances and a vacancy in a church or club. A departing editor takes away all that plus the potential for a long-term perspective of the community, dedication to improvement of a place, and the subtleties of local knowledge and history that underlie the community dynamic.

Transience chills passions about place and time. The allure of better jobs at larger places meant that the journalist had no lasting stake in the community and so the problems in the current town need not be resolved, only reported on. Success at that was the key to the next step. This growing mobility reinforced not only the concept but also the practical usefulness of professional detachment, which was confused with objectivity in the minds of most journalists.

Therein lies a conundrum. Although journalists as individuals cannot realistically be much different from anyone else in society, we operate out of a philosophical notion about detachment that declares a very large difference. (The pun in the conundrum: "Our difference is indifference.")

Journalists rationalize the artifice of detachment as necessary to do the job of reporting news. How, the rhetorical question goes, can we report honestly and credibly about affairs without being removed from them? The trap is that although we can try to hold ourselves removed, we cannot in fact be removed; we are unavoidably caught up in the tides of societal, political, and technological change and the results of that change, and the way we go about our work unavoidably affects public life.

When the reporter or editor arrives at a new post, he or she might bring little or no local knowledge, but the traveling case includes that deceptive old friend detachment, which, the philosophy contends, could by itself make the journalist effective in any situation in any place: the difference of indifference as panacea.

It doesn't work that way, of course. The culture of detachment dictates that the transient journalist may make no real impression on local public life even if he or she did understand the stakes, for to try to make an impact would be to sacrifice a perceived professional obligation. In the 1970s and 1980s, that shield from reality insured that newly mobile journalists, their eyes on the next rung of the ladder, worried little about whether things went well in their latest and temporary environment. Helping things go well wasn't in the job description.

Movement, however, was. Annual turnover of 15% to 25% in newspaper staffs was not unusual. Television's turnover, tied to numbers reflecting even small differences in stations' market size, was even higher. A reporter's move from a 48th-ranked market to a 35th might make no substantial difference except on his or her resume, but it was a step toward the ultimate goal—the network.

Failure to move in 2 or 3 years was equated with career stagnation. Even at the level of editor and other top executives, the steamrolling expansion of chains such as Knight–Ridder, Gannett, Thompson and others created a demand at newly acquired properties. As one link in the chain moved, others inexorably followed. With only 1,700 or so daily newspapers, top editor changes over a decade or less would affect a large percentage of that relatively small congregation and the communities they served.

CAUGHT UP IN IT ALL

Inevitably, I became part of that transience. In 1970, after 12 years at the *Observer* including one, 1969, as its Washington Bureau reporter, we moved to Boca Raton, Florida where I would be editor of Knight Newspapers' 9,000 circulation, 5-day-a-week newspaper with a staff of eight, two of them reporters. Why? Because it was there. Because my years in Charlotte and Washington had convinced me that helping five people to do five stories was personally more rewarding than doing one myself; because it was 1970 and upward mobility was an ache in the belly and a spur in the hindquarters.

At 34, I would have My Own Show. And, as I quickly discovered, it most assuredly was My Own. When the sports editor (who was, of course, the entire sports staff) went on vacation for 2 weeks, I was sports editor. Same with the photo editor and women's editor (also, of course, one-person staffs.) Their vacations were carefully timed not only not to overlap, but to be well-spaced so that I might actually be editor for a few weeks between filling in at their desks.

Twenty months of that regime in a sleepy village of 22,000 with about 75% unemployment (read: retirees) and a distressingly high component of reclusive millionaires was quite enough. So when Knight Newspapers decided to expand its Washington bureau and create the job of news editor under Bureau Chief Robert Boyd, I eagerly fled back to the capital, and a new editor moved in to tell the news to Boca Raton.

As the five of us drove back up I-95 that March of 1972, more change was in the air than our latest address. The ever-contradictory Nixon was just back from his "journey for peace" in China while all his men were deep into planning for the 1972 reelection campaign; Vice-President Spiro Agnew was enraging the press corps with railings about "nattering nabobs of negativism"; and Senator George McGovern of South Dakota was on the way to the Democratic nomination and thinking about vice-presidential choices. All of that was flavorful grist for the Washington media mills; so much news to be told.

In just over 2 thunderous years, they would all be gone: Nixon and all his men, Agnew, McGovern, and his eventual vice-presidential choice, Senator Thomas Eagleton of Missouri. Journalism would have passed through Watergate and into a new, and perilous, era.

THE EAGLETON AFFAIR

John S. Knight, III, grandson of Jack Knight and his heir apparent to the Knight Newspapers fortune since Johnny's father's death in World War II, was an editorial writer at the *Detroit Free Press*. In July, only days after McGovern named Senator Thomas Eagleton of Missouri as his vice-presidential running mate, the younger Knight called me at the bureau.

"Probably nothing to this," he said, "but I thought I'd better pass it along and let you decide. I had a call from a political person here who says that Eagleton has had serious psychological problems and has had shock treatments for them in the past. You might want to check around."

Clark Hoyt of the national reporting staff was in St. Louis to work on a profile of the relatively unknown Eagleton, a routine part of the postconvention process that turned out to be well beyond routine. Combing through the files of the *St. Louis Post-Dispatch* for anything about the senator, he noted a strange pattern during Eagleton's years as state attorney general in the 1960s. He would be much in the news, then suddenly disappear. In one instance, a small item said that he had been to the Mayo Clinic for "a check up." Another time, he had been treated at Johns Hopkins "for exhaustion." Hoyt made notes to ask about those episodes when he got to the point of interviewing Eagleton.

Meanwhile, Knight's tipster called again, this time with the name of a doctor he said had been present at an electroshock treatment. The doctor, a woman no longer in practice, lived in an exclusive gated community in St. Louis. Fortunately for Hoyt, no guard was on duty on the Sunday he drove out. She answered the door. He introduced himself and said he wanted to talk with her about the time in 1964 when she had been present for electroshock treatment of Eagleton at Barnes Hospital.

"Her faced turned white," Hoyt later recalled, "her jaw literally dropped. As she closed the door she said 'I can't talk about that.' It was clearly true, but clearly unusable" (C. Hoyt, personal communication, July 1994). Hoyt and Boyd were convinced that they had the story, that Eagleton had indeed been hospitalized for shock treatments connected to serious depressions, but there were no medical records, no confirmation, nothing printable.

McGovern and his staff, with a horde of reporters, had retreated to the Black Hills of South Dakota to plan for the struggle against Nixon and Agnew. Boyd and Hoyt decided to approach Frank Mankiewicz, McGovern's press secretary. They showed him Hoyt's circumstantial memo and said they wanted to talk with Eagleton and see his medical records. All, of course, very privately, to protect their story. Mankiewicz acted stunned by the memo, but actually already knew about the problem because his office had also received calls from Knight's tipster. In fact, Eagleton had already been urgently and secretly summoned to the Black Hills for a confrontation.

Mankiewicz stalled Boyd and Hoyt for a couple of days, then announced a press conference for July 25. The reporters feared the worst, and it happened. Eagleton announced to the assembled press corps that on "three occasions in my life I have voluntarily gone into hospitals as a result of nervous exhaustion and fatigue." McGovern closed the press conference by expressing confidence in Eagleton's present health, and the next day extended that with the ill-fated pledge of being "1,000 percent for Tom Eagleton, and I have no intention of dropping him from the ticket."

While Mankiewicz was giving away their carefully reported and responsibly handled exclusive, the two frustrated reporters were huddled under a table in the press room dictating their version to the bureau. Their restraint had a bitter taste as it was shoved down their throats. As a consolation prize, Mankiewicz persuaded Eagleton to talk with Boyd and Hoyt on the ride from the Black Hills retreat to the Rapid City airport. Yes, Eagleton told them, McGovern's people had asked him the traditional question about skeletons in the closet and yes, he said, he had withheld the medical information. Over the next 6 days, McGovern's "1,000 percent" support melted in the heat of endless questions and speculations. On July 31, Eagleton withdrew from the ticket. Whatever slim chance McGovern had against the Nixon juggernaut evaporated.

Critical ethical questions swirled around the resignation: Were the medical treatments relevant, given that Eagleton had performed his senatorial duties apparently unimpeded since 1969? Should a person with a history of severe depression when under pressure be second in line with his hand on the nuclear trigger? Was Eagleton's coverup (a prophetic term in light of the next year of Watergate) his real sin, not the illness itself?

There were also critical journalistic questions: Had Boyd and Hoyt, in an excess of caution, tossed away a major exclusive by insisting on total confirmation, or had they been rigorously responsible? Was the tip to Johnny Knight just another dirty trick by the Nixon crowd? Did that matter, because it turned out to be true? Was it better to have the revelation come against Eagleton the candidate rather than against Eagleton the vice-president? Was the journalistic responsibility to tell the news and let the public decide? Is that what happened?

Although some of those questions arose immediately around the Eagleton affair, the debate did not run for long. The news had been told. Boyd and Hoyt deservedly won the Pulitzer Prize for national reporting, which nevertheless inspired one Washington cynic to note that it was "the first time anybody ever won a Pulitzer for a story they didn't write."

For me, the Eagleton case was clear cut. The medical facts were true and spoke to his ability to perform under pressure. Eagleton provided no medical report or doctor to say that the underlying causes had been removed. As Hoyt said, "By every test of private information that I know, this affected his ability to perform in office" and thus needed to be known (personal communication, March 1994).

The Eagleton affair, however legitimate and responsibly handled, opened a journalistic door to less legitimate matters less responsibly handled. In light of later events—Watergate, Agnew's disgrace, Edmund Muskie's tears, Gary Hart's meanderings, Bill Clinton's bimbo eruptions, Clarence Thomas and Anita Hill's disagreement—the tough issues of intent, character, candor, and responsibility have become even more complex and universal. Journalists played visible and active roles in each of those notorious events, and the debates over them by the public at large added to the increasing unease Americans feel about the content and motivation of what they read and see in the news.

As surveys in the late 1970s and 1980s consistently showed a loss of credibility by journalists, we wrote it off as the burden of being the messenger. If we are mired far down in the trust ratings alongside politicians and aluminum siding salesmen, we told ourselves, it's simply because they don't understand. They really do want us to tell them the news; it's the news they don't like, not us.

That was not correct. They really did not like us, and the wound was self-inflicted. The increasingly high profile of political reporters, their constant appearances on television shows as pundits rather than reporters, the unceasing self-promotion of star anchors by television networks and local outlets, and the fawning celluloid celebration of the Watergate journalists began to meld politicians and political journalists into an amorphous and distant they. Journalists and politicians looked and often acted like a cohesive establishment of elites: imbued with insider status; playing by arcane rules and keeping score with irrelevancies; seemingly indifferent, if not impervious, to outside challenge. Neither group seemed to relate to the lives of average citizens and neither was reflective of their desires, ambitions, or values.

Something to Think About

If journalists insist that the artifice of detachment limits us only to reflecting events, then our credibility in writing about public affairs is forever tied to the judgments, manipulations, and credibility of a politics gone bad. Hating the message of politics inevitably equates with hating the messengers of it.

JOURNALISM AND POLITICS: RELUCTANT SYMBIOSIS

Symbiosis is two dissimilar organisms living in a mutually beneficial relationship, each bringing something essential to the whole. If either partner changes too radically too suddenly, it kills the other and thus itself. If one organism becomes too similar to the other, if something bordering on assimilation occurs, the relationship loses the benefits of difference. Likewise, if one organism becomes too different from the other, the relationship loses the benefits of commonality. Either way, both lose the benefits of symbiosis and die.

A healthy symbiosis between politics and journalism is essential and life sustaining not only for them both but also for a third entity: democracy. When the symbiotic relationship falls ill, so does democracy.

This concept becomes clear when one considers the relationship between politics and journalism in a situation in which the political sector dominates and controls the press. The assimilation of the press into the body of government makes democracy impossible. On the other hand, if journalism is not attentive to the activities of government, democracy also becomes unviable. As with much of life in a democracy, it is a matter of appropriate balance, and in the testy arena of politics and journalism, that balance is delicate and ever-shifting. The proper involvement of people in governing themsleves depends on that balance being maintained. If for no other reason than that, journalists need to see their role as more than the mere provision of information.

Nowhere is the symbiosis of politics and journalism more complex and the partners' concern about the relationship more uneasy than at the White House. The president and the White House press corps are virtual captives of one another. There are periodic efforts on the part of the White House to break out: Clinton's early-term stabs at going directly to people through town meetings; Nixon's (and his successors') gatherings of beyond-the-beltway editors at the White House for personal briefings closed to the regular White House press corps. The White House press strives mightily to break out by developing sources in the administration but outside its formal press apparatus.

After I left Washington for the editorship of the *Wichita Eagle*, I was regularly invited to what the White House press corps disdainfully called those "country editor briefings" with the president. More to feel the personalities than in expectation of picking up a meaningful story, I attended such sessions with presidents Carter and Reagan. Predictably, no news resulted, but the unease in the White House press corps was palpable, as mine had been when, as news editor of the Washington bureau, I knew such "get around the Washington press corps" sessions were going on.

Clearly, the president is not going to announce world war or proclaim peace or resign at such a gathering. But Washington journalists (and I was one) worried that those provincials (and I was also one of those) would miss some nuance of speech, some hidden corner of policy declaration that could constitute, by their definition, news.

When transcripts of the sessions were released to the White House troops hours after the meetings, they were parsed and participled, read like entrails of a sacrificial goat, in a search for meaning too obtuse or subtle for the provincials to have grasped. It is not recorded that any story of any level of importance ever emerged from one of those sessions, but the regular press corps' unease arises each time one is held.

Despite such occasional end-run efforts, the President's normal route to the public is through the 60 or so regular White House reporters, and their route to information about the president's activity and thinking is through the president and the people in the White House. That is where the symbiosis begins.

The press corps, or at least a representative pool of reporters, is allowed to go wherever the president goes, whether across Pennsylvania Avenue to Blair House or around the world. No law makes that so. The president could simply leave on Air Force One anytime he choose. He could say to the press corps, "You're not going," leaving it to the reporters to try to figure out where he is headed and get there on their own, if they

could. That just does not happen, and the fact that it doesn't illustrates
the fundamental nature of the symbiotic relationship.

The foundational principle for the relationship, on which both
partners agree, is that the American people have a right to know, at
the very minimum, that the president they chose is alive and function-
ing. What he is doing, how he is doing it, and who he is doing it with
are merely enhancing details that the press corps wants but that can
be given or withheld by the White House at its discretion. Because the
relationship works both ways, however, the White House knows that
it cannot starve the press corps for information without paying a price
in public image, leaking sources, and personal relationships. Thus,
the reluctant partners exist by living off of one another, each trying to
use the other to maximum benefit while avoiding domination by the
other.

The synapses of the relationship are complex, although Washington
insiders prefer to call them sophisticated. The connections sometimes
short-circuit, resulting in pure confusion on the part of the people who
reporters are supposed to be informing.

A good example of problems in the arcane coding of White House
coverage came in May 1994 as President Clinton sought to fill a
Supreme Court vacancy. Clinton's reputation even from his days as
governor of Arkansas was one of taking a long time to make decisions.
Whether the cause was actual indecisiveness or a contemplative,
careful weighing of possible outcomes and political implications was
irrelevant by the time he was inaugurated. Journalists, who must
make many decisions instantly, have a low tolerance for contemplation; it doesn't make good copy. So by April of his second year in office,
deservedly or not, he was labeled as wishy-washy and every action or
inaction was interpreted in that light.

In situations such as pending presidential appointments, several
conventions of the symbiotic relationship come into play.

On the reporters' side:

- Every reporter wants the story first. Being the first to raise the
  name of the eventual appointee wins kudos from the boss and
  garners drinks at the press club.
- Surfacing a name allows the reporter to develop several more
  stories, warm with the spice of conflict, by bouncing the name
  around Capitol Hill and special-interest groups to get reaction,
  usually negative.

In each case, the information is attributed to one of a variety of
spectral beings who float through the rooms of the White House: an
administration source, a White House staffer, a highly placed spokes-
person. Each of whom, of course, declined to be identified. All of that

chasing around is mostly irrelevant to average citizens, who would be happy not to think much about the issue until the president actually names someone. Given the confirmation process, there is plenty of time for people to make their views known without wasting time on ghost appointees floating on trial balloons.

On the White House side:

- Sometimes the president or his staff wants to float a name or two to test the waters. The reportorial reflexes mentioned earlier are totally dependable for getting that done. So a staffer leaks a name to a favored reporter, and the game is under way. Both the reporter and the source know the name of the game, that each is using the other. It is symbiosis at work.
- Sometimes a presidential staffer wants to appear to be in the know, or, for other reasons of self-interest, wants to leak a name to a favored reporter. (In a couple of the more Machiavellian versions of this convention, a staffer will find an indirect way to drop a totally unlikely name to an unfavored reporter, who then gets egg on the face, or a pretender manages to get his or her name into the mix.)

So on most appointments, as with the May Supreme Court one, the air is full of speculations, opinions, rumors, and controversy. Everybody involved in the symbiotic relationship is getting a fix off all the turmoil, and, at one level, that is the game. In many cases, there is no real harm done to the public.

Occasionally, however, the wires really get crossed, and the public is misled, as in the May Supreme Court nomination of Judge Stephen Breyer to replace the retiring Harry Blackmun. Here's how Public Broadcasting System's Nina Totenberg described the process to her national audience:

> The praise greeting the Breyer nomination will undoubtedly detract from the peculiar public twisting and turning that the president took in reaching his decision. Early this week, Mr. Clinton was said to have chosen Interior Secretary Babbitt, but Republicans then threatened to fight. The president switched to Judge Arnold, but women senators were displeased by some of the judge's opinions on women's rights issues. And so, in the end, the president made the safe and consensus choice. For some, it was a sign of presidential weakness that he did not stick with his own instincts. But for others, it was the system as it should be—a model for presidential consultation with Congress."

For the record, it should be noted that Clinton himself had said absolutely nothing in public or to journalists about any of the three until he announced his choice. Totenberg has been a well-respected reporter around Washington for a long time, and she knows how the game is played. Her commentary, however, reflected none of it. It merely hung Clinton with the waffling label.

So strong is the symbiosis, however, that even a president will not risk damaging it. In finally announcing the nomination, Clinton talked about the difficulty of the decision, and in a departure from convention talked about why he did not nominate two other people whose names had been bandied about for weeks, with first one name being the journalists' hot bet, then the other.

It is instructive concerning this symbiosis to look carefully at the words used at that press conference after the president completed his statement:

Question: Mr. President, why, in the end, do you think there was so much—maybe it's our fault as much as it is your aides' fault—but why was there so much confusion in which direction you were leaning? Earlier in the week, we thought that Secretary Babbitt had the best chance, then later *it was* Judge Arnold, and now, of course, you've made your decision?

(Note the interchangeable pronouns: you, we, it. What is going on here?)

Clinton: Well, because you all didn't talk to me. When we have these appointments that only I make ... with all respect to my aides, I think I know as much or more about it as they do. ... I care a lot about the Supreme Court. I read people's opinions. I read articles. I read letters that people send me about prospective candidates. I think about this a lot and I care very deeply about it. And I was going to take whatever time I had to take to think this through. (italics added)

Although clearly annoyed with the implications about his alleged indecisiveness in the question, Clinton passed up the opportunity to take a harder shot at the complex interplay of aides and journalists and leaks and self-interested unattributed sources that had wound up casting him as wishy-washy.

To thoughtful citizens who struggle with difficult decisions of their own, the exchange must have sounded otherworldly. Of course they want the president to work hard at such decisions, and, of course, only the president knows where his head is at any given time. Yet the implication of the question and the reporting on the press conference was that the president had waffled his way, at last, to a decision.

Historians and reporters who think of themselves as writing history on the run will complain that the public has a right to know the process and background of important presidential decisions. That is a valid point, but in this case, and most similar ones, the process and background are only half told. An arcane notion about objectivity and distance requires that the part about the symbiosis—the role of the reporters in the process—be left out. The president's alleged indecisiveness becomes a convenient shortcut to avoid writing the truth.

In this case, both partners in the symbiosis suffered in the eyes of outsiders. The journalists seemed judgmental, the politician indecisive. The truth, as messy as it is, would better serve the ends of public life and the acceptance of both journalism and government.

MAKING SYMBIOSIS WORK

The symbiotic relationship between journalism and government exists at every level and in every place. Each needs the other; each uses the other. Each is, and should be, wary of distortions in the relationship.

In the early 1960s, Mecklenburg County, where Charlotte is located, was hiring its first full-time, professional county manager, a substantial change in local government. As the appointment would be announced at a Monday morning meeting, my county beat competitor at the afternoon *Charlotte News* would get the story first for his Monday afternoon edition unless I was able to break it over the weekend, ahead of the meeting. Both of us had written speculative stories during the weeks of maneuvering over the appointment and had become personally interested in figuring out ahead of the other just what would happen. Our "on the one hand ... but on the other" interpretive efforts to corner the story ahead of time led one commissioner, Charlie Lowe, to sit us down and spin one of the cracker homilies for which he was locally famous:

> You fellas remind me of the story of the speculative dog. Goes like this:
>
> Now, IF you had a dog.
>
> And IF he ate sand.
>
> And IF it was a hot day.
>
> And IF you gave him water.
>
> And IF you ran him around a lot.
>
> And IF he had a square anus.

Then he MIGHT pass a brick.

But you got to have all those things together. That's what you fellas do, string all those "ifs" together and come out with square dog doo. What's the point?

I didn't have a good answer for Charlie, but I did have a good hunch that the choice would be the county manager from Guilford County, North Carolina. However, getting Lowe or anyone else to confirm it seemed impossible because the commissioners had sworn each other to secrecy. City Editor L. M. Wright's menacing, "I want that story first" was providing me with extra, fear-based incentive as the week neared its end and the story was still unwritten.

On Friday before the Monday announcement meeting, I told one commissioner (not Lowe) with whom I had developed a reasonable relationship, and who not incidentally was up for reelection, that I felt strongly it would be Guilford's Harry Weatherley. He would not confirm it, even off the record. He needed the help of the other commissioners in the coming election more than he needed to help me, and he feared it would be clear, if he confirmed my hunch, that he was the source. However, he also saw his stake in keeping me as happy as possible, so he said if I could find a second source and prove to him that I had by getting some piece of new information from that source, I should call him on Sunday and he would confirm. Not for attribution, of course.

I knew that another commissioner, a rural member getting along in years, was in the habit of a Sunday afternoon nap, and that his wife was a garrulous, friendly sort. I waited until I was sure the commissioner was well into his nap, then called the house.

"Is Mr. Frank in?"

"Yes, but he's taking a nap. Want me to wake him?"

"Oh, no, don't do that. I just want to talk with him about Mr. Weatherley and the meeting tomorrow morning."

"Oh, that's all arranged," she kindly volunteered. "Mr. Frank will make the motion and Hank will second it. Want me to have Mr. Frank call you?"

"Oh, no thanks. That's all right."

Gleefully I called the first commissioner and told him who was going to do what the next morning.

"Well, I don't know how you got that, but it's right," he said.

The story led the *Observer's* front page on Monday morning, the rival *News* was vanquished, City Editor L. M. Wright was in an unaccustomed good mood, and all was right with my world. The symbiosis worked for its own internal purposes. It was a clean exclusive, and we at the *Observer* proudly considered it the height of what we were supposed to be about.

Of course, the only benefit to the public was that it learned of the appointment 4 hours earlier than it would have otherwise. In this case, no harm was done to the public or the process, but is that a sufficient standard?

Something to Think About

The ultimate beneficiary of the symbiotic relationship should be not one or both of the partners but a well-functioning political life in which people feel included and, therefore, which they do not hate.

❖ F I V E ❖

The Limits of Toughness

We knew the call would come to disrupt our family vacation in the North Carolina mountains, it was simply a question of when. Libby and I had packed ourselves and three kids for a week and driven from summer-sultry, tense Washington to enjoy fresh air and plain food with her parents in the house they had assembled with their own hands from huge, interlocking logs taken from abandoned 150-year-old cabins. From their mountain above Valle Crucis, our prospects were a little fishing in the cold, swift Watauga River, lots of walking, and visits to the clapboard, two-story, slightly listing Mast Store where locals played mountain music on weekends and you bought live chickens for dinner out of the coop under the trap door in the middle of the ancient wooden structure.

We left behind a city, a government, and a press corps writhing in crisis. Watergate was clearly rushing toward denouement after more than a year of unmatched intensity in a city whose psychic temperature runs in the red numbers even in the most placid of years.

Not a particularly good time for the news editor of the Knight Newspapers Washington Bureau to leave, but then, there had not been a good time for that in 18 months as hundreds of Washington reporters struggled to keep pace with the *Washington Post's* thunderous revelations about Richard Nixon's White House crowd.

The plan was for Bureau Chief Robert Boyd to call if there was a major break and for me to rush back. He did, saying something was imminent, and I did, flying into Washington National late on a warm, misty August night in 1974.

The cab ride to the National Press Building to check into the bureau and the one-block walk down F Street to the Washington Hotel where we kept a room was eerie. Familiar landmarks seemed coated in something more foreboding than the diffused sparkles from the light rain. Bassins, the sidewalk cafe that hunkered at Pennsylvania and 14th where the J. W. Marriott now towers, was dark, its red-and-blue umbrellas celebrating Cinzano folded for the night. The vacant, pigeon-

60

filled Willard Hotel, since transformed into a $300-a-night palace for the beautiful people and lobbyists, slumped in glum abandonment, its broken windows staring vacantly over Pennsylvania Avenue.

My thoughts were as opaque and changing as the drizzled cityscape. Two blocks west, at 1600 Pennsylvania Avenue, Richard Nixon was making a decision. Later, we would learn, he had knelt on the floor in prayer with Henry Kissinger. That night, however, few of us who had struggled with Watergate could have imagined such a scene. Rumors of Nixon-summoned tanks in the street, of an unprecedented constitutional crisis after months of stonewalling were far more current than rationality would support.

The outdoor bar atop the Washington Hotel looks westward across the Treasury Building right into the windows of the White House's east wing. Sitting there, I could hear a steady blatting of car horns as drivers responded to pickets outside the iron White House fence carrying signs reading, "Honk If You Think He's Guilty."

It was time for The Big One in journalistic terms, the running to the ground of a strong, elusive, determined and dangerous prey. Surely the kill was near, but a cornered bear is the most dangerous bear, and fear of a less-than-peaceful surrender was palpable. Staring at the White House through the misty rain, I recognized that my profession had changed in a fundamental way over the past 18 months. The natural and useful arm's-length, symbiotic relationship between journalism and government had dissolved into all-out war. Perhaps it was unavoidable, for the nation had elected a president and advisers of unprecedented singlemindedness. Convinced of their rectitude in all matters and caught up in a culture of machismo, Nixon and his men let neither truth nor law stand between them and their aims. It was they who had compiled the enemies list, tapped reporters' telephones, dissembled on the simplest of matters, perfected the vocabulary of "stonewalling" and "modified limited hangout" and "twisting in the wind," tried to suppress the Pentagon Papers, devised the political dirty tricks and paid G. Gordon Liddy for them, and used the presidency not as a bully pulpit but a billy club. If there had been a declaration in that all-out war, it had come from 1600 Pennsylvania Avenue, not the National Press Building two blocks East. If the watchdog had become the attack dog, it was through provocation, I decided.

The tanks did not appear, of course. The constitutional crisis did not overflow. On August 9, Richard Nixon read a statement, walked stiffly to a helicopter on the south lawn, and flew out of a presidency unparalleled in its ambiguity.

There was, however, little emotional ambiguity for journalists in the weeks and months that followed. We celebrated. We were not celebrating the departure of Richard Nixon the political figure; we were celebrating the reaffirmation of the intent of the First Amendment: that even a runaway administration of enormous power and guile could be called to account by tough, determined and free reporting. We didn't know then that something else, something dangerous, had occurred.

POST-WATERGATE SYNDROME

The resolution of Watergate was an extraordinary moment in U.S. history. It was also a pivotal moment in journalism and in public life, for the initial reaffirmation of the First Amendment quickly deteriorated into an era just as threatening to public life as had been the election of the Nixon crowd.

What should have been a plateau from which the profession moved on to even greater heights turned out to be a peak. From it, we viewed all below us as territory ready to be subjected to a transmogrification, in all that word's negative aspects: the journalist as folk hero, the astute political analyst as media star.

For journalism, the heady rush of bringing down a president gave way to a two-decade post-Watergate syndrome that molded generations of journalists, their readers, their news sources, and American politics itself. Suddenly, journalism schools were overflowing and newsrooms were superheated by the feverish belief that if one cannot bring down a president, a dog-catcher isn't bad for starters. Seeing Richard Nixon as prototype rather than anomaly, journalists began treating all political figures at any level as suspects in the next Whatever-Gate. The sewer commissioner who drives his county-owned car to the grocery store at night isn't G. Gordon Liddy, but, hey, we do the best we can with the material at hand.

The journalistic norm became, "We catch crooks." Small-bore Whatever-Gates won the profession's plaudits and awards. Scalps on the belt, particularly government scalps, were the sign of rank and the measure of testosterone at gatherings of the tribe. The democratic process, superbly served by the Watergate reporting, was devalued by the onslaught of self-indulgent journalists-cum-cops.

Our internal reward system—the bestowing of plaques and the garnering of fame and bigger jobs—assured that a pinched, shortsighted version of valid and important investigative reporting became the norm. It moved from catching crooks in government to superficial exploration of everything that was a problem—that is, everything negative—about the society, from AIDS to zebra extinction. We labeled the chorus of alarums "agenda setting" and "consciousness raising" and, indeed, many instances of superb reporting led to significant changes in public processes, including government. That was not new to journalism. Post-Watergate, however, the standards gradually eroded. As the watchdog mutated into the attack dog, the worst aspects of journalism's embedded cultural traits became magnified. For every brilliant bullseye, there were multitudes of misfires that left large piles of individual and institutional casualties. A high percentage of the exposes merely exposed, with no suggestion about solutions. Like amateur exploratory brain surgery, inexpert and contextless investigative reporting left rather a mess.

But everybody was doing it, and the onslaught pushed the public further into the grasp of Postman's (1985) discontinuity, for much of the zealous reporting "answered no question [they] had asked and ... in any case, did not permit the right of reply" (p. 68). But journalists were full of self-importance, fulfilled in what we saw as our natural and singular calling: the relentless uncovering of wrongdoing, no matter its ultimate importance either to the public or the great scheme of things.

Not surprisingly, the self-reinforcing emphasis on killer journalism coincided with a decline in consumer appreciation of the effort. As we rushed about catching crooks large and small, the public's regard for journalists declined almost in proportion to the energy we expended.

A great deal of the investigative reporting—both hits and misses—necessarily involved government and political figures, most often portraying them as one-dimensional, clumsy, or mendacious in what they did, or, alternatively, as doing nothing. Americans already forced increasingly inward by societal pressures found it tempting and easy to turn off both politics and journalism. Our agenda setting was, to many of them, simply all that negative news because it seemed to be without purpose other than to expose. Some people simply did not believe the stories; others tuned out in disgust or frustration, believing that if things were indeed that bad, remedies were not in their grasp.

Our ways of presenting the catalogue of alleged sins put the public in the role of bemused, at best, but, more likely, disgusted spectator. Politics became the machinations of an unreachable *them*, written about by equally unreachable journalists. So journalists and public officials, viewed equally if inaccurately as partners in the problem, came to be ranked along with aluminum-siding and used-car salesmen in the public's list of people who can be trusted or deserve to be attended to.

Inevitably, in the post-Watergate years journalism's toughness—put another way, its chronic cynicism—began to approach its useful limits: debate as confrontation, campaigns as horse races, compromise as caving-in, intellectual growth as waffling, reticence or lack of knowledge as cover-up, conflict as the most valued journalistic coin. In short, public life as spectacle. Examples? One need not dig too deeply:

- Note the vocabulary of journalism in virtually any newspaper or broadcast, before and after a presidential debate: showdown, tactics, pivotal, who won—who lost. Who angered whom or who scored the most points dominates over issue clarification or nuance.
- Notice the vocabulary of campaign reportage. In 1988, for instance, 82% of the wrapups (the closing lines of a story) by correspondents on the three broadcast evening news shows focused on horse-race themes—that is, on campaign strategy and tactics, on the effectiveness of campaign techniques rather than issues (Hallin, 1992).
- Hear the managing editor of CNN News at a seminar on political coverage: "It really doesn't matter who runs against Clinton next time. He's going to be running against our tape library." Every public word the president utters is on tape, that editor was saying, and if he says something different next time, we'll nail him. What passes for a hard-nosed accountability campaign, however, also precludes the possibility of political growth. If the penalty for learning, for adapting to changed circumstances, is being nailed forever to the past, will anything or anyone ever improve? "Read my lips: No new taxes!" first helped make George Bush president, then made him the target of attack and the butt of cynical jokes as, inevitably and wisely, taxes were raised for important purposes.
- Listen to the conversation of a very good, and very tough, reporter:"I can write all the policy stories in the world, all the balanced, on-the-one-hand-on-the-other stuff, but the stories I hear about, the ones people call pissed off about, are when the mayor and somebody are yelling at each other. Conflict is what people love and get excited about, so I give 'em conflict. We're nothing if we're not read, and that's what people read."

Public life as spectacle. Toughness as the ultimate virtue. The post-Watergate syndrome had other important effects:

- The relentless search for the next Watergate necessarily turned politicians into stereotyped targets in the minds of many journalists. Increasing numbers of people inclined to enter public life, particularly politics, decided it was not worth the grief imposed by cynical and suspicious journalists. Automatic challenge of their motives and the attribution of innate slyness, if not mendacity, repelled even the most well-intentioned. That trend of discouragement left the political field to those less well-intentioned, which only reinforced the stereotype in the mind of journalists and, ultimately, the public.

- The relentless exhibition of toughness for its own sake, displayed nightly on television and daily in newspapers, inevitably distorted public attitudes toward the democratic process. If a Sam Donaldson, before millions of viewers, could turn cynicism and boorishness into a professional virtue, why should an ordinary citizen feel restrained in attitude or expression? If every public figure was subject to less than civil treatment, if shouting became synonymous with debate, if the crisp quip served as well as thoughtfulness, why should people at large act any differently?

Something to Think About

It is interesting that journalism's binding axiom of objectivity allows, even requires, unlimited toughness as a tool as well as a credo, yet it rejects purposefulness—having a motivation beyond mere exposure—as unprofessional. Without purposefulness, toughness is mere self-indulgence.

TWO FACES OF TOUGHNESS

Almost 10 years after Richard Nixon's resignation, in the spring of 1984, the nation's newspaper editors saw two new faces of toughness—one of purposefulness, one of self-indulgence. Nixon, busily trying to construct an image of senior statesman, was invited to speak at a luncheon of the American Society of Newspaper Editors' (ASNE) annual convention in Washington. He had not addressed such a gathering since his "I am not a crook" statement in 1973.

The ASNE lunches, often addressed by sitting presidents and other headline figures, routinely draw several hundred editors and spouses, clustered at tables of 10. Nearly 1,000 such guests were gathered that day in the Sheraton-Washington ballroom for Nixon's return to face his former tormentors, the people he said he could not be angry with "because you can't be angry with someone you don't respect." Among them, ensconced at the *Washington Post's* customary center-front table was Ben Bradlee, the consummate Watergate tough guy; the editor who helped it all happen. Bradlee seemed in his usual high spirits, table-hopping with wife Sally Quinn as America's newspaper editors filled the room with chatter and expectation.

After lunch, as the editors shuffled their chairs to face the still-empty stage, Bradlee and Quinn arose at their center-ring table that was now the focus of a thousand pairs of eyes. Leading their tablemates, they wound their way half the length of the great hall and out the double doors, leaving a starkly empty table directly in front of where Nixon would stand.

If Nixon was aware of the demonstration by the *Post* people, he gave no sign as he took the stage to warm applause by the remaining editors. Standing on a bare stage with only a single floor mike, with no intervening or protective podium, no lectern for support or shelter, without notes or other aids, he delivered a brilliant 45-minute lecture on foreign policy and domestic politics. It was an astonishing, nearly inhuman display of grit, the man with perhaps the greatest burden of public humiliation possible facing, totally without physical or psychic protection, hundreds of those who participated in his humiliation.

Absent, of course, were the people from the *Post*. At the time that they paraded out of the luncheon, the phrase that crossed my mind was "bush league." Time has tempered that judgment, however. I see it now as merely sad; a display of congenital journalistic toughness for its own sake.

TRUE TOUGHNESS

The ultimate tough story, the ultimate scandal, is that America's public life does not accomplish the long-term goals of the American people.

Barlett and Steele (1992) of the *Philadelphia Inquirer* uncovered a large piece of that scandal in their epic 1991 series and 1992 book *America: What Went Wrong?* Tens of thousands of everyday citizens saw themselves reflected in those pieces about the economic destruction of the middle class, and, in an era of alleged disconnectedness, more than 25,000 of them responded personally to the reporters.

Many of them, Steele said in a 1994 interview, noted that "the first step for fixing something is to know what's wrong, and you told us that and we thank you."

That series began as a look at plant closings and their impact on people. When the reporters had finished months of research and interviewing the people affected, a clear and forbidding pattern began to emerge.

Steele's words in the interview, carefully selected, were cautiously in the traditional journalistic mode:

> We felt that some specific ... public policy decisions had been made, particularly from a tax standpoint and regulatory standpoint that were clearly impacting very negatively on middle class jobs. ... We saw a breakdown in public policy, an inability for public policy makers to see what was happening.

Did they, at some point during the months of reporting, begin to develop a sense of purposefulness? Again, no admission:

We feel that if you're able to pull together available information and show someone a picture of that which they didn't know or fully understand, you have served the purpose. You have illuminated a corner of public policy and public understanding of an issue that previously didn't have light on it. To show the full magnitude of it and the drama of it, to us that is a service.

Their newspaper series did not include suggestions about solutions, but their book does.

Few news organizations have reporters to match Barlett and Steele and fewer yet could devote the resources to support such a pair. The most pressing need, however, is not for more *America: What Went Wrong?* epics, as fine as it was. The need is to make the sort of purposefulness that series demonstrated (despite Steele's denials of purposefulness) an accepted part of the newsroom culture.

Discussion of the idea of purposefulness among a group of journalists almost always leads to someone's suggesting that the answer lies in more toughness. "Isn't it just a matter of good old hard-nosed reporting, asking the really tough questions?" is a typical challenge.

As theater, that might work; or as a demonstration of journalistic machismo. Finally, however, tougher and tougher questioning without purpose other than to confront and illuminate conflict provides only the sort of spectacle that alienates all sides, including the citizen-consumer of the information produced.

True toughness does not reside simply in relentless grilling of actors on the public stage—elected officials, institutional leaders, advocates of an action or a point of view—although such questioning is a necessary part of journalism. Neither does it lie in a posture of cynicism. Its core resides in journalists accepting the fact that what we do has a direct effect on how public life goes and disciplining ourselves to forego the attractions of episodic, superficial reporting on events and moving on to purposefully dealing with the underlying processes of democracy.

Something To Think About

Superficial toughness for its own sake has its limits as a cultural trait and can easily betray its users. It needs something more: purposefulness in terms of a concern that public life go well. Then toughness becomes a vehicle and not a destination.

❖ S I X ❖

Connect and Disconnections

We were back on the North Carolina mountaintop in June 1975, and the view was hazy. Watergate had come and gone and Gerald Ford was house-sitting the presidency abdicated by Nixon. Washington seemed to be settling back into normal operations as the world's largest company town, grinding out its annual quota of laws, debates, and mini-sensations over issues that seemed to never move any closer to resolution.

The prospect of several more years, or an entire career, of dealing in that atmosphere was not appealing to me. A bureau's job, after all, is limited to offering stories that you hope newspapers will have the good sense to print; whether they do so or not is totally out of your hands. Sometimes it was as if we merely lobbed shells out into a vacuum. For me, there was no real product; no chance, at the end of the day, to hold in my hand something as satisfyingly palpable as a newspaper that I had made.

Libby and I talked much about that as we sat on the mountaintop; about long-term ambitions and about The Merger. In 1974, Knight Newspapers and Ridder Publications had completed an odd-couple sort of union—the Knight papers, widely known for their news orientation, and the Ridder papers, widely known for competent business operations, constituting Knight–Ridder, then the nation's largest group in terms of daily circulation, with 35 newspapers coast to coast. For me, at 39, it was, in the vernacular of the hustling 1970s, midlife crisis time.

The saving phone call came while we were in the mountains mulling over those things. Derick Daniels, vice-president for news of the merged company, asked if I was interested in talking about the editorship of two newspapers in Wichita, Kansas. I was clearly interested in talking about the editorship of any newspaper, but Wichita was a cipher; to a life-long East Coaster, an unknown in one of those filler states lying between Washington and the West Coast. The unease about place was not lifted when we picked up the only immediately available reference material in the mountain house—a 1940s encyclopedia. Its piece on Kansas began: "While Kansas has produced no notable people. ... " By summer's end, however, the five of us had packed up and driven West.

Why? Because it was there, and because I remained convinced that helping five people to do five stories was personally more rewarding than doing one myself. Because it was 1975 and upward mobility was still an ache in the belly and a spur in the hindquarters.

Once again, I would have My Own Show, and it was a real show this time, morning (the *Eagle*) and afternoon (the *Beacon*) newspapers with a combined Sunday circulation of 180,000 and news staff of 160. Wichita would be an important consummation of the Knight–Ridder merger, a Knight editor and a Ridder publisher bringing their contrasting cultures to the same newspapers for the first time. I looked on that as opportunity, despite this last-minute admonition from Byron Harless, the new company's personnel wizard: "You summbitch, you better make this work."

It would be, I figured, a building job of 3 to 5 years, then off to other challenges. I knew how to tell the news and could help other people to do it. That's what it was all about, wasn't it?

TELLING THE NEWS, ENDLESSLY

In that summer of 1975, newspapers and television news were seeing only a few small shadows of clouds on an otherwise still-sunny landscape. Although it was true that the percentage of U.S. households receiving a newspaper was down slightly, total circulation and readership were rising steadily. For television, it would be two more years before the first negative blip on the ratings screen. The Baby Boomers, the postwar population bulge, were the ones forming all those new households and they were approaching the age, the mid-30s, when, historically, people became avid newspaper readers. That they might not follow the historic trend was hinted at in some surveys, but we were convinced that was simply delayed maturation, that it would be only a matter of time before they, in middle age, were captured by the newspaper habit.

All that was needed was to tell the news, and we had new journalistic tools for doing it. Investigative reporting was being institutionalized as a specialty, with its own national association and with the imprimatur of a Pulitzer Prize in that category. Reporters could step out of the role of purely observing to provide background and analysis pieces, of course properly identified as such. Computers were coming into their own as ways of finding and manipulating complex data.

In television, cities were being strung with cable, providing multiple channels of information hard-wired into home sets. In Europe, companies were experimenting with computer-based interactive communication, and by the end of the decade, Knight–Ridder would be deeply involved in an experiment in this country.

Toffler's (1981) Third Wave was crashing against journalism's seawall. For 200 years, U.S. journalism had been a constantly growing mass, first manifesting itself in newspapers, then broadcasting and magazines. In the mid-1970s, however, as Toffler noted, societal change and technologically competitive forces were eroding that mass. He labeled it "the de-massified media" (p. 155).

Potential audiences for traditional mass journalism were becoming fragmented not only by competition from new technologies but also by changes in lifestyles: more two-parent families in which both held outside jobs, sharply limiting time for reading and viewing; more single-parent families; and a drive for economic success that took priority over other matters.

Into this unpromising mix we were pouring more information gathered from more places by more sophisticated technologies. We were continuing to build Postman's (1985) "world of fragments and discontinuities" (p. 68), and much of the news was bad: disturbing events over which people felt no control, frustrating events that begged for public response but lacked any visible handles, and threatening events that invited retreat into the security of narrowed lives. What felt to us like the providing of useful information at a higher and higher level was in fact creating disconnections, and by almost every measure since the last half of the 1970s, the disconnections are real and growing.

Our first response to the eroding numbers was to spend countless hours and dollars analyzing the declines and devising ways to chase down readers in their manifold and ever-changing life niches. Demographics, psychographics, weather graphics, shorter stories, redesigns, and reader involvement were among the vehicles brought into the chase. The assumption behind all the effort was that readers had changed in some fundamental, fathomable way that we could respond to directly if only we could define the change. Even if we could have accurately identified the change, however, our response would necessarily have been to tailor the journalistic product to whatever those changes appeared to be at the moment and stand prepared to change again and again with each apparent permutation of the public psyche. We were treating people as consumers to be sought, as potential readers or at-risk readers; as a commodity rather than as a public.

Something To Think About

Consider for a moment that the real problem is not that people change (for they surely do), but that journalists do not; that we do not know how to resonate with the public's changes, or don't care to. In short, that people are forced into Postman's nether -world because they cannot find themselves, their real concerns, and their values reflected in the crush of news that we thrust on them. What are the implications of that proposition?

TELLING THE NEWS IN WICHITA

Such theorizing was of little concern to me in August 1975. The new editor of the *Wichita Eagle* and the *Wichita Beacon* had some rebuilding to do. In 1959, *Time* magazine referred to Wichita as the "bottom of the barrel" of journalism because of the bloody and public scandal mongering between the two families that owned the then-competing newspapers, the Murdocks at the *Eagle* and the Levands at the *Beacon*.

"Trying to outdo each other in sensationalism," *Time* wrote, "they reach desperately for banner headlines, inflate insignificant news, and spend most of their time shrieking at each other, e.g., TOP EXECUTIVES OF EAGLE BRANDED AS LEADERS OF ABORTIVE POLITICAL PLOT."

Time continued, "When a girl [sic] staffer at the *Beacon* shot herself, the *Eagle* tried to associate a Levand with the case. A rumor that a Murdock relative was homosexual caused the *Beacon* to campaign for an ordinance to require the registration and fingerprinting of every pervert in town." And it was 1959, not 1859.

That period of journalistic excess ended early in the 1960s when the Murdock family, owners of the *Eagle*, bought out the Levand family. However, another dramatic change in the Wichita scene came in 1973 when Ridder Publications bought both newspapers. The *Eagle-Beacon* was then operated by Britt Brown, great-grandson of founder Marshall Murdock. Brown owned the largest block of stock and other family members held the remaining shares.

Brown, said to be weary of family feuding over the newspapers, asked his lawyer, Paul Kitch, to negotiate a sale to one of the many newspaper companies then on the prowl. Meanwhile, Brown set out to improve the papers' bottom lines, a time remembered by long-time staffers as "the scorched earth policy." Through firings, severe cutbacks on news space and coverage, a ban on investigative reporting (announced to the public in a front-page editorial), and discouragement of more talented staffers, the financial picture improved to the point that Ridder Publications eventually paid more than $42 million, an enormous premium even in those days of runaway bidding for local newspapers. The price, newspaper analyst Lee Dirks would testify in a suit over proceeds of the sale, was the highest cash price ever paid for a newspaper operation.

The price, Dirks said, probably justified the $1.2 million finder's fee paid to Kitch and the 10-year, $65,000 annual employment contract for Brown. Other stock-owning family members and a local bank did not agree, however, because both men who benefited had been on the board of directors and had not told the others about their personal stakes. The minority stockholders filed a long-running lawsuit that eventually resulted in Kitch's having to include his finder's fee as part of the sales price.

But the damage was done. With the merger the following year, Knight–Ridder inherited Wichita newspapers in disarray, the staff depleted and dispirited, the papers' reputations tarnished. Only a few days into classes at his new high school, our older son asked plaintively, "Dad, when people ask me what you do, do I have to tell them you work at the newspaper?"

"Nope," I said, "tell them I play piano in a whorehouse."

I set a lofty goal for the first 2 years—not to be embarrassed twice a day by my newspapers. This was not the fault of the people in the newsroom or the several hundred other employees. They struggled under impossible conditions of pay, morale, and lack of a vision for their newspapers. The way I would avoid being embarrassed, I felt confident, would be to simply tell the news honestly, accurately, and as fully as possible. After all, that was the job, wasn't it?

Given that start to my Wichita adventure, it was doubly satisfying when, in 1984, *Time's* 10-year survey of the nation's best newspapers included the *Eagle* as being among "the best of the rest ... newspapers that are too small to ever qualify for the ten-best list but which vigorously pursue issues in their communities" (Time, 1984, p. 62).

In the years between 1975 and 1990, we filled the walls of a large conference room with the symbols of journalistic accolade—plaques and certificates and honors from national and regional competitions for investigative work, for writing and photography and layout, for public service reporting and editorial writing, sports pages, and features. Still the downward drift in readership and circulation continued, and the problems we investigated in 1976 were still around in 1986 and, without fundamental changes, likely would be in 1996 and 2006.

By traditional measures, we were telling the news at a high level, but not much was happening. With the rest of the nation, Wichita was discovering that the problems of the last half of the 20th century were problems not of ignorance about the situations that existed but lassitude about fixing them. Focused on material advancement in an

unpredictable economy, weary from the crush of contextless information and alarums, wary of institutions large and small, cynical even
about cynicism, Wichitans, like most Americans, seemed unable to
summon the will and cooperativeness to deal with the most basic
problems. By the end of the 1980s, most surveys showed that people
had little hope that things would improve; certainly they exhibited only
limited capacity for making them better.

CREATING DISCONNECTIONS

Much of the fault, I believe, lies with those of us who were so relentlessly
telling the news but missing something crucial. We were, in fact,
creating a series of disconnections between ourselves and the public,
in the public, and between the public and institutions. The inevitable
result was ennui and drift in public life.

The disconnections we were unknowingly causing fall into three
broad areas: failure to understand how the public decides about
issues, journalists' "trained incapacity" (the phrase is Jay Rosen's,
personal communication, 1993) to recognize the need for and value of
true public deliberation and how it arises, and the shortcomings of
episodic reporting of news.

HOW THE PUBLIC DECIDES

The routine, accepted conventions of telling the news, far from helping
resolve important issues, can in themselves cause a disconnection in
the process of public life. To explore this territory, it is important to
understand how the public makes up its mind on issues. Yankelovich
(1991) clearly outlined a multistage movement to what he called public
judgment.

Public judgment, the point at which actual resolution of an issue
can occur, is "the state of highly developed public opinion that exists
once people have engaged an issue, considered it from all sides,
understood the choices it leads to, and accepted the full consequences
of the choices they make" (p. 6). It is a far more advanced state than
mere opinion.

The process begins with raised consciousness, the public's becoming aware that a problem or issue exists. Journalists are expert at
consciousness raising. We call it agenda setting, and it is apparently
so self-satisfying that we dash around raising consciousness here,
raising consciousness there, then rush on to raise consciousness
somewhere else, leaving all previous crises unattended and unresolved. When those hummingbird-like efforts fail to also provide some

framework by which citizens can think about and begin to grapple with the issue, when our efforts merely describe a problem seemingly beyond a citizen's reach, the result can only be frustration for those citizens. It is not surprising that much of the public wearily shrugs off what journalists feel is important, tough agenda-setting reporting as simply "all that negative news."

True resolution of problems, according to Yankelovich (1991), requires more than mere raised consciousness, or public opinion. It requires a period of working through. This involves the public realizing that the problem must in fact be resolved; dealing with second thoughts; adapting to new, perhaps unwelcomed, realities; and, finally, sorting out and compromising competing core values. The result is democratic consent.

The first step, raised consciousness, can be virtually instantaneous, requiring only the time it takes to transmit a piece of information, or it can be a slow realization. The second step, working through, invariably takes some amount of time for consideration and discussion. It often takes years. Compare that reality of how the public decides against how journalists reflect the process back to the public.

"The problem with newspapering," the editor's hoary lament goes, "is that it is so damn daily." In the world of CNN and its competitors, the lament might be "the problem with broadcast is that it is so damn hourly" or even "so damn instantly." The impatient and unrealistic journalistic model of public life is that it moves quickly and directly from consciousness raising to resolution. Or, at least, that it should move that way. That, of course, ignores the necessary and often time-consuming working-through phase.

Journalists whose daily, hourly, instant efforts ignore the working-through imperative are destined to miss connecting with the public because the reporting presents an unrealistic, instant-answer world of experts and absolutes in which the average person cannot find oneself or one's beliefs.

Take almost any contentious issue. In the name of balance, we call on experts, one on each side, who, in order to meet our perceived need for balance, appetite for conflict, and hunger for resolution, must be absolutists. Equivocation may be reflective of the real world, but it makes for bad copy. Thus the promising middle ground of compromise, the area that reflects what reasonable people might think or want to do about an issue, rarely surfaces in our reporting.

On most issues, most people harbor some ambivalence, so when journalists or politicians portray the choices in absolutes and insist on instant resolution, people do not see themselves as part of the discussion. "If that's what it's about," they reason, "my views aren't in this discussion." As they have little chance to insert their views, they simply opt out of the discussion altogether, declaring a plague on both houses—and on the journalists who portrayed the issue in those terms.

For example, it took 7 years for the Brady Bill to become law. The renewed push for a waiting period on handgun purchases came shortly after President Reagan and James Brady, his assistant, were shot in 1981. Over those 7 years, the debate was portrayed by journalists as a tug between gun control advocates and Second Amendment absolutists and between conservatives and liberals; at stake was the determination of political winners and losers and all that was needed to resolve it was a conclusive vote in Congress.

Journalists are not alone, of course, in the false framing of the issue. As Dionne, Jr. (1992) convincingly demonstrated in *Why Americans Hate Politics*, politicians, for their own narrow purposes, frame issues in false extremes. In fact, journalists' relentless focus on the process of politics rather than its content legitimizes and reinforces that sort of behavior in politicians. Our narrow focus allows their false framing to work.

At one level—a superficial one—we were merely telling the news by reflecting that absolutist-based distortion of reality in the Brady Bill debate. While that unending, never-changing polarized debate was playing daily in the newspaper and nightly on television, however, citizens were intuitively following Yankelovich's (1991) template, working through the issue's parts, factoring in new realities such as alarmingly increased gun violence, and bouncing those realities off their values system. Finally, a critical mass of public willingness to compromise on core values surfaced and was communicated to Congress, and the bill became law.

Right up until the ink was dry on the new law, newspapers and television portrayed the struggle as a battle of extremists and the making of political winners and losers, considerations that, in fact, never entered into most people's thinking about the issue. Rather, a majority of people had reached judgment because they had "considered it from all sides, understood the choices it leads to, and accepted the full consequences" of the choice. A substantial majority of Americans had decided that Second Amendment absolutism, some additional trouble in buying a gun, and the possibility that the law was a step down a slippery gun-control slope were outweighed by the possibility that lives might be saved.

Note that the arrival at public judgment involved a sophisticated and difficult balancing of core values. At the poles of the issue were the right to bear arms and public safety. However, the individual decisions turned on many additional subtleties and subtexts, and the long weighing process involved, in Yankelovich's (1991) terms, the balancing of emotional, cognitive, and moral factors.

Gallup Polls indicated that the public was making a fine distinction between the Brady Bill specifically and gun laws in general. For almost two decades, through 1993, support for stricter firearms laws averaged about 66%, swinging between a one-time low of 60% (in 1986) and a high of 78% (in 1990). Likewise, those favoring handgun registration moved, from 66% in 1982 to 81% in 1993. Support for the Brady Bill, however, first surveyed in 1988, held at around 90% right through those years.

Locked into our focus on politicians, experts, and absolutists as the source of our reporting, we were not attentive to, and did not reflect back to the public, the deliberative process that was going on.

Something to Think About

Had the Brady bill working through process occurred 40 years ago, 8 in 10 of the Americans involved in the deliberation would have been basing their views on what they read, primarily in newspapers. In 1990, barely 6 in 10 adults were newspaper readers, and only 2 in 10 trusted what they read. Isn't that a self-inflicted wound?

TRAINED INCAPACITY AND "THE SWAMP"

Much of the public's working through on the Brady Bill, as with most issues, occurred out of sight, deep in a place that David Mathews (1993) of The Kettering Foundation compared to the swamps of his native South.

The swamps were viewed for decades as places of little value, a region of snakes and 'gators, strange noises, mosquitoes, and bad smells. When waterside property became scarce, it occurred to some people to fill in the swamps and build condominiums, shopping centers, and housing developments, superimposing their notion of usefulness on what they felt was a useless, smelly mess.

Of course, what we now accept as inevitable happened. The fish in the bays began to disappear, the shrimp became scarce, and the water turned foul. Something elemental and microbiologically crucial that we could not see and would not have found very attractive had been going on in the swamp and we had interfered with it. We began to learn lessons of ecology.

Mathews made a comparison to a cultural ecology that has a swamp of its own, a fundamental place where public issues first arise and brew in a conversational stewpot of opinion, rumor, fact, and conjecture. The messy but crucial cultural process of that swamp is also endangered. Journalists, either ignorant of its importance or intellectually fastidious about its messiness (Rosen's trained incapacity), avoid that swamp. Instead, we focus coverage of public affairs on formal, safe, visible governmental structures and easy-to-reach experts. Just as failure to understand and honor the dynamics of the physical swamp endangered the overall environment, failure to know and understand the dynamics of the cultural swamp endangers the democratic environment.

Our journalistic vision of public life is almost always one of clear division: on the one hand, government, the political side, as initiator, prime mover, deliberator, decision maker; on the other, separate, unconnected, probably inconsequential and certainly transient activities by ordinary citizens in pursuit of what matters to them. Citizens' specialized, fragmented, targeted aims make them hard to see at times, and some of their goals strike us as quixotic or parochial when they are comprehensible at all.

The cultural swamp, however, is crucial to the total democratic environment. The first iterations of ideas and opinions that ultimately are translated into political issues and decisions are often spawned in the swamp. Concerns about crime, for instance, do not originate with a city council, they bubble up to it. Certainly, worries about ever-rising taxes are not initiated in legislatures, they grow out of the swamp. When we are focused on the reactor—government—rather than the activator—people—we are missing an important connection.

Our view of the way things work, and therefore the view that our reporting unavoidably projects, is simplistic: government as the actor to which we need to be attentive; people as the acted on, who we might occasionally ask to comment but who otherwise have no role. This is democracy writ backwards, but our inability to see the public as actor is nearly complete, so in ways large and small we signal to citizens that they have no role in public life other than a reactive one.

As journalistic routines such as the narrow focus on government become ways of seeing the world that are particular to journalists, they also become ways of not seeing. A strictured and symbiotic world of government, politics, and journalism comes to exist on its own, without regard to the people being affected by the relationship.

We have developed a second "Great Concrete Momma"—the buildings of government. Limiting our world view to the newspaper office and the governmental structures protects us from the swamp and reinforces our incapacity to imagine much beyond those walls. That trained ignorance of the smelly cultural swamp makes things seem more coherent and efficient, and it is a more comfortable mode for us to operate in. Some crucial products of the cultural swamp suffer, however, just like the shrimp in the biological one.

Ignoring the realities of the swamp gives rise to more than a broadly inaccurate view of reality:

- It creates yet another disconnect between journalists and citizens. Once again, the issue is people experiencing one reality in their lives and seeing a vastly different, and therefore less believable, version reflected back to them by journalism. We project our trained incapacity onto the public, and, frustrated, they hate it, grow more cynical about government, and distrust us.
- It neglects an opportunity to use our considerable reinforcing power to encourage more citizen participation.
- It reinforces the idea that political life and the rest of life are not connected.
- It encourages politicians to continue operating under their own set of rules written with their self-interest in mind.

With the swamp analogy in mind, Richard Harwood of Harwood & Associates set out in 1995, at my request, to map the cultural swamp of one typical city, Wichita. His findings from 18 months of experimentation and research were reported in "Tapping Civic Life," published by the Pew Charitable Trusts. The workbook offers journalists clear guidelines for discovering in their communities how and where issues first begin to arise. The reporting methods outlined can add richness and vigor to the coverage of public affairs.

Something to Think About

The swamp of real life isn't an attractive or easy place to operate. But ignoring or abusing it won't work either. Revitalizing public life means accepting the reality that the swamp is a critical part of the total democratic environment. All aspects of public life are connected, even if in sometimes tenuous ways, and we must not only acknowledge that but actively find ways to cultivate the totality.

EPISODIC REPORTING

If we are to help revitalize public life and find our place in it, we must understand the public not as consumers or spectators but as potential actors. Revitalization requires places for true deliberation to occur and an information flow designed to move the discussion along. It means framing issues more broadly than as an either/or situation; taking the risk, if there is risk, but certainly the burden of moving beyond the politicians' polarized formulations.

Neuman, Just and Crigler (1992) called this constructionism. One could simply call it good reporting, but of a different kind: reporting with the purpose of advancing debate as opposed to merely passing along information.

Their book, *Common Knowledge*, reported on an in-depth study of five major issues and citizen responses to media coverage of those issues. The study led them to conclude that on issues of high salience, that is, issues that the subjects said were of personal importance to them, "especially those [issues] having a long agenda history, the press may play a very different role, drawing attention to new solutions, multiperspectival views, historical context, or economic impact." When that occurs, they contended, journalists are "more effective in the democratic process" (p. 119).

Their interviews, they wrote:

> Suggest that at least part of the public's limited interest in the official side of national and international affairs results from a profound sense of powerlessness. Ironically, the ... style of what is usually considered journalism at its best may reinforce this sense of powerlessness through an emphasis on irony ... or ... the hopeless complexity of issues. Our subjects reacted with special enthusiasm to information on how to take control of issues. (p. 111)

Toffler's (1981) cautionary perspective on de-massified media also suggests the need for more than a bipolar approach to problem solving. He, too, blamed the political system for perpetuating the doctrine of false choices:

> Today, the very complexity of issues inherently provides a greater variety of bargainable points. Yet the political system is not structured to take advantage of this fact. Potential alliances and trades go unnoticed—thus unnecessarily raising tensions between groups while further straining and overloading existing political institutions. (p. 424)

It is true that the political system is not structured to take advantage of that "greater variety of bargainable points," and it is equally true that the journalistic system that tells people about the politics is not structured to do so, either. The notion of detachment stands in the way.

Another disconnection, another frayed spot in the fabric of public life grows out of our efforts to overpersonalize the news, to lure back our departing audiences by humanizing large issues. Believing our audience to be unable or unwilling to deal with broad issues, we set out to make them easy by particularizing. Using personal anecdotes to illustrate larger issues can be effective, but when the anecdotes constitute the entire story, when the underlying issues are never properly addressed, as too often happens, the device backfires in some interesting and important ways.

One of the unintended consequences of anecdotal presentation is its impact on how Americans view political accountability. The phenomenon is stunningly documented by the University of California–Los Angeles' Iyengar (1991) and reported in his book *Is Anyone Responsible?* The thrust of his findings is that the fast-paced, anecdotal, " ... and now, this ... " style of news presentation favored by broadcasters—because they are convinced it produces ratings—also gives political figures a free pass from accountability.

His detailed studies of Americans' reactions to televised news stories uncovered consistently distinct responses to two different types of presentation—those that are episodic and those that are thematic. Episodic presentation is typically what television people think of as hot—a snippet of an unemployed individual, for instance, portrayed in his poor surroundings, talking briefly about his unemployment as a way of illustrating and personalizing an economic problem. Thematic presentation is what television people deride as talking heads, a more thoroughgoing discussion of unemployment and its underlying economic causes, perhaps by a panel or through in-depth reporting.

Most television people love episodic presentation. They view the hot 20-second sound bite with the jobless person as holding the politicos' feet to the fire by showing a slice of real life to illustrate failed policy. It's a gotcha. Politicians hate it for the same reason. As an embattled President Reagan complained to the *Daily Oklahoman*:

> You can't turn on the evening news without seeing that they're going to interview someone else who has lost his job. Is it news that some fellow in South Succotash has just been laid off and that he should be interviewed nationwide? ("Television News Angers Reagan," 1982, p. 1)

Iyengar's (1991) research indicates that, far from complaining, Reagan and his fellow politicians "should actively encourage more South Succotash stories" (p. 138). The reason is that when Americans see such anecdotal stories, they particularize to the person or event involved. They don't make the leap between the man from South Succotash and chronic, underlying economic problems; rather, they see such people's fate as "mere idiosyncratic outcomes" (p. 137). They may even blame him. More importantly, they "settle upon causes and treatments that 'fit' the observed problem" (p. 137) that is, that man should get a job, or shave or wear a better shirt rather than laying responsibility at the feet of society or political leaders.

Americans can, however, deal with underlying issues when properly presented. In fact, when the thematic (the much-disparaged talking heads) presentation is used on the very same issue, Iyenger's studies show, the reaction is just the opposite: People make the connection with underlying causes and, therefore, assign responsibility to the system and the political decision makers behind the system. The distinct reactions are consistent across income, education, and ideological lines.

Because of this, Iyengar (1991) concluded:

> Episodic framing contributes to the trivialization of public discourse and the erosion of electoral accountability. ... The portrayal of recurring issues as unrelated events prevents the public from cumulating evidence toward any logical, ultimate consequence. By diverting attention from societal and governmental responsibility, episodic framing glosses over national problems and allows public officials to ignore problems whose remedies entail burdens on their constituents. Television news may well prove to be the opiate of American society. (p. 143)

Television journalists complain, with at least some foundation in fact, that it's the nature of the beast. Time constraints, money, audience rating points that generate advertising revenue, good pictures, and real people are basic to the business, they contend. If those are, in fact, the immutable truths of television news, then the unavoidable conclusion from Iyengar's research is that good television makes for bad public life.

The question for television journalists, however, must be whether all of those hard realities are, in fact, real.

Certainly local television news everywhere acts as if those truths are immutable. A traveler staying at a Holiday Inn that looks just like all the other Holiday Inns calls out to the nearby mall that looks and smells like all the other malls for a Pizza Hut pizza from a place that looks like all Pizza Huts and produces a formula pizza available everywhere, and sits down to watch local television news that looks, sounds, and feels the same in Omaha as New York as San Francisco as Waco: Two white males and a blonde woman, all between 25 and 38, are packaged and paced and primped in the same way; fungible assets in a stylized burst of chatter quieted only occasionally by a furrowed brow to indicate something serious might have happened but bothering you only for 90 seconds about it because you might turn away.

"But," TV traditionalists complain, "it works. And the alternative is too dreary to contemplate—a show with people sitting around talking about a serious matter and expecting people to watch for more than 2 minutes without flipping over to ESPN."

The fact that it works statistically may be akin to the well-established phenomenon of a hot new fishing lure. Somebody catches a lot of fish one day with the "Li'l Darlin'." Word spreads, so more people buy that lure and fish with it. Soon, everyone is fishing only with that lure, so, of course, it catches even more fish for a while. But sooner or later, the realization sets in that the same number of fish are being caught as always. The fish, as fish will, were just eating what was there, and "Li'l Darlin'" was there the most. So it worked.

If the standards of telling the news were based in concern for public life going well, all news would look very different. For instance, if the objective of public affairs reporting were to hold public officials accountable in a meaningful way, we would see and read a lot less of South Succotash and hear a lot more about underlying issues.

THE CHALLENGE: CAN WE HANDLE CHANGE?

Dionne (1992), in a new afterword to the Touchstone edition of *Why Americans Hate Politics* wrote, "Americans want a politics they don't have to hate. And therein lies our hope: Democracies are uniquely open to change, and if citizens want politicians to move beyond false choices, it is in their power to demand it" (p. 373).

If he is correct, as the growing citizen restiveness of the 1990s indicates he may be, journalism clearly has both opportunity and challenge. The anger, the incipient revolt against politics and journalism, needs an outlet and invites a useful response by journalists. Can we repair the three disconnections by understanding how the public decides about issues and reflecting that in our reporting, by recognizing the need of true public deliberation and how it arises, by moving beyond the episodic reporting of news?

Something to Think About

If Americans are, in fact, ready to demand change in the politics of false choices, journalists will unavoidably either abet or hinder the change, whether we intend to, want to, or are comfortable with that role. Will our role be as central to the rejuvenation of public life as it has been in its deterioration? What would have to change to make that happen?

❖ S E V E N ❖

Making a Break

Unlike North Carolina, Kansas has no mountaintops to raise the level of late-night contemplation, but the openness, the wind, and the big sky have the same elevating effect.

Over the years, Libby and I have added two decks to the Wichita home into which we moved in 1975. The south one serves for fall and early spring evenings when the chill wind is still out of the north and provides a sunny shelter on crisp winter afternoons. The north one works in summer, protecting from the hot south winds but allowing a good view of sprinting thunderstorms and a chunk of prairie sky.

Dinners on these decks often turn into midnight conversations about this and that, our voices blending with the constant low rustle of breeze through the elm trees. Those are our times and places for sorting things out, the talk ranging from the delights of kids and grandkids to budget struggles with corporate headquarters to Wichita's leadership problems to more cosmic concerns. The mood on the north deck one warm night in August 1990 was somber. A desultory contest for governor was getting under way between Democrat Joan Finney and incumbent Republican Mike Hayden. The agony of developing yet another newsroom budget in austere circumstances was a nagging wraith. The city seemed mired in endless and unresolved wrangling about taxes and services, and the local economy was uncertain. Teenagers were shooting one another with increasing regularity. The media continued to decline in authority and credibility. Fifteen years of telling the news in Wichita seemed, in the depths of that evening, to have little meaning and provide less reward and, for me as an editor, at least another 15 years of dealing with such matters lay ahead.

Two years earlier, in 1988, barely half (50.1%) of America's potential voters had turned out to pick George Bush over Michael Dukakis, the lowest turnout in 64 years. Those who voted did so after a campaign in which the enduring images were of a skulking Willie Horton, Bush in a flag factory, and Dukakis grinning goofily from an armored vehicle,

the oversized helmet making him look like one of those wobbly headed
sports dolls on the dashboard of a pickup truck.

On November 13, a week after the dreary 1988 campaign, I had
written in an op-ed column:

> The Constitution requires that we do it again in four years whether we
> need it or want it, and that's not a pretty thought as we stand in the
> shambles of the 1988 presidential race and contemplate the threat of
> another one sometime soon.
>
> The dreary thought has nothing to do with who won or lost the presi-
> dency. Rather it has to do with the nature of the campaign, the perform-
> ance of journalists and candidates in it, and what those say about the
> future of the election process. ...
>
> The campaign just concluded showed at its frustrating worst the mutual
> bond of expediency that has formed over the years between campaigns
> and the media, particularly television. Together they have learned that
> feeding the lowest common appetite among the voters is safer, cheaper,
> and less demanding than running the risk, for the campaigns, and the
> expense, for the media, of providing in-depth information.
>
> The hard truth that journalists and their organizations face is that the
> campaign people aren't going to change simply because it would be right
> to do so. The campaigns have learned they can produce results without
> risk. So changing the contract is up to the media. (Merritt, 1988, p. 15A)

Some suggestions for rewriting the contract followed, including:
take the risk of boring readers and viewers; stop participating in
so-called debates that are actually shams; abjure sloganeering and,
instead, focus on positions, even if they arrive in those deathly dull
position papers; and clean up the horse race polling act. Not a
spectacularly heady agenda, but a start.

Other journalistic voices were saying similar things that winter, as
at least some proportion of people in the profession looked back in
revulsion on what had occurred.

DEVELOPING A DIFFERENT WAY

The 1990 Kansas gubernatorial race was shaping up to be more of the
same—a dreary enough prospect for me that August night, even
without the other, equally dreary circumstances. Incumbent Hayden,
and challenger Finney, with 18 years as elected state treasurer, had
won the summer primaries. The campaigns in the Kansas heat were
carefully managed into simplemindedness. Hayden had talked about
providing more of the same, without saying what that might be, and
Finney had gripped-and-grinned her way across the state's 400 miles

without ever taking a stand on any issue except an oracular claim of "hearing the Voice of The People."

One of them was going to get more votes than the other, assuming that anybody at all voted. We would cover the whole affair as if it actually had meaning, and, 4 years later, with the state facing the same set of problems, two more people would run and one of them would be elected by avoiding any talk about real solutions.

The politicians' part of the electoral process certainly would not change. The public would not, on its own, change without knowing the possibilities that change could open. That left only one part of the formula—ours.

The next week, I wrote:

> In the interest of disclosure as the 1990 Kansas gubernatorial campaign begins, I announce that the *Eagle* has a strong bias. The bias is that we believe the voters are entitled to have the candidates talk about the issues in depth. (Merritt, 1990, p. 13A)

I outlined a general coverage philosophy whose thrust was to insist that the candidates address the issues, whether or not their own strategy was to do so. We would be aggressive—insistent—about that.

> If our insistence ... winds up seeming to cost one or the other votes, so be it. I am perfectly comfortable defending the notion that you as a voter have the right to know what the candidates intend to do once in office, and if the candidates won't say what they intend to do, letting you know that very plainly. ... What the eventual winner intends to do with the great gift that voters will bestow is a straightforward question that deserves a clear answer. (p. 13A)

Other journalists in other places were thinking along similar lines. In an eerie coincidence, my phone rang just as I was doing the final editing on the piece quoted here. Glenn Guzzo, then assistant to Knight–Ridder Vice–President of News Jennie Buckner (now editor of the *Charlotte Observer*), was shopping around an idea. K–R, he said, was looking for a newspaper willing to try new approaches to election coverage to see if the alarming trends in voter turnout and issueless campaigns could be affected. K–R would provide resources beyond the normal budget, including money to research the efficacy of the effort. You've come to the right place, I said.

Managing Editor Steven A. Smith took charge of what became known internally as "the voter project" and in the paper as "Your Vote Counts." The thrust of the plan was a straightforward, unabashed campaign to revive voter interest backed by total focus on the issues that voters were concerned about as reflected in survey results. Recognizing that the newspaper reached only a portion of the population, we enlisted the ABC affiliate KAKE-TV as a partner.

The 8-week campaign was chronicled by Smith in a series of reports that became a sort of early textbook on reformed campaign coverage and was distributed to other newspapers at their request. Some snapshots from our journey down a new road deserve mention:

- Early in the process, I ran into a well-traveled friend in her 70s whose intelligence and insight I admired. "Why, you're trying to save democracy, aren't you," she observed. I modestly agreed with that assessment.
- A startling insight occurred midway through as we struggled to pin down the candidates on issues. Abortion was a major one, and Finney's congenital, rambling abstruseness was making it impossible to understand her position. In frustration, we printed verbatim a press conference answer that was, in fact, incoherent. Outrage steamed from the Finney camp that we would quote exactly what she said; they howled that it was unfair. The campaign later provided a translation, of sorts, although even that "position" was full of ambiguity.
- A set piece of the project was a Sunday issues box in which we detailed the candidates' positions and noted any changes. It ate up two thirds of a page. Initially, the campaigns were not interested enough to talk about the content, assuming it was a one-shot effort that would go away. When it did not—because we ran it every Sunday—they became intensely interested in how their positions were detailed week after week.
- Postelection surveying confirmed our initial hunch that people wanted candidates to address the issues. Of the array of things that we did, two were deemed most useful by a majority of respondents: the weekly issues box and the in-depth explorations of issues. Daily campaign coverage, horse-race polls, and columns extolling the virtues of voting ranked far down their usefulness list.
- There were two substantive results: Voter turnout was up across the state, but more so in areas where our coverage was available; voter cognizance of issues was strikingly higher in our readership area than elsewhere in the state.
- Finney won; a perverse outcome considering that Hayden was far clearer on the issues. However, voters in Kansas and across the country were in a strong anti-incumbent mood and were determined to throw the bastards out, and Hayden simply could not overcome that burden. By 1994, as Finney's term neared an end, Kansas Democrats and Republicans generally agreed that she was the most ineffective governor in recent history. Lined up to succeed her was a field of a dozen, at least eight of whom were the strongest candidates for that office in at least 40 years.

Something intriguing and promising had happened. We had delib-
erately broken out of the passive and increasingly detrimental conventions of election coverage. We had, in effect, left the press box and
gotten down on the field, not as a contestant but as a fair-minded
participant with an open and expressed interest in the process going
well. It had involved risk (as I told Libby on the deck that night, "This
may cost me my job"), but it had paid off.

It was also a liberating moment, for me and for the journalists at
the *Eagle*. We no longer had to be victims, along with the public, of a
politics gone sour. We had a new purposefulness: revitalizing a mori-
bund public process.

The 1990 election breakthrough set other things in motion, in
Wichita and elsewhere. In the spring of 1991 we used lessons
learned in 1990, added some twists, and did similar activist coverage for local elections—a sort of off-season exercise for 1992's big
year. By then, there was plenty of company. Steve Smith's report on
our 1990 efforts had been widely circulated, both in Knight–Ridder
and outside. Other newspapers, most notably the Charlotte Observer, and institutions, most notably the Kettering Foundation and
The Poynter Institute, were approaching 1992's elections with new
ideas. Poynter and the Observer combined in a sophisticated effort
of asking citizens what issues they were concerned about, developing ways to pin down the candidates on those issues as well as the
issues raised by the candidates.

The Observer's efforts also changed some of the chemistry of the
failing symbiotic relationship between campaigns and journalism:

- The *Observer* asked, in the Senate primary, for the candidates'
  positions on environmental issues. Incumbent Senator Terry
  Sanford's campaign refused. *Observer* Editor Rich Oppel relayed
  a conversation in which the senator insisted, "We don't intend to
  talk about the environment until the general election. That's part
  of our strategy." Oppel told him, in effect, the people want to know
  now, and we're going to talk about it now, whether you want to
  participate or not. We'll just run white space under your picture.
  The campaign provided the information.
- *Observer* reporters, at first ill at ease in doing so, asked questions
  at press conferences such as, "Mrs. Emily Smith of Monroe wants
  to know ... ?" Competing reporters at first looked on askance,
  but the *Observer* reporters grew to appreciate the device. Candidates could not dismiss Mrs. Smith's question as readily as they
  might a reporter's, so they responded with care.
- During its survey of 1,000 people, the *Observer* had asked if the
  respondents—not all of whom were readers—would be willing to

serve on a voter panel throughout the campaign. Five hundred citizens leapt at the chance to have a continuing voice.

By most accounts, inside and outside the profession, journalism's performance in the 1992 presidential election was substantially better than 1988, despite Gennifer Flowers and a few other distractions. Not everybody got it, but clearly a journalistic rebellion against the abuses of 1988 was under way.

Even with the distractions, Democratic candidate Bill Clinton clung to his expressed intention to talk about issues. As the challenger, of course, that was to his advantage at a time of broad concern over the economy, health care, crime, and other core issues. He laid out, in excruciating detail ("Putting People First"), what he would do if elected. He developed ways to get over and around traditional campaign coverage through appearances on talk shows, at public forums and in paid "town meetings."

President Bush ran a slogan-oriented, traditional campaign. Ross Perot, the third-party spoiler, aggressively appealed to what he saw as middle-American concerns and spouted snappy one-liners about the economy. He carved out 18% of the vote. Bush had 37%. Clinton was a minority winner with 42%. Importantly, voter participation was 55.9%, a substantial increase over 1988, and a reversal of a decades-long trend.

As planning for 1994 began, more journalists were starting to get it. National Public Radio was mounting an intensive project nationwide in cooperation with local newspapers. In Florida, a coalition of the state's largest newspapers was coming together to share resources in an effort to focus campaigns there on issues. Dozens of newspapers, including the Boston *Globe* and the San Francisco *Chronicle*, redrafted their 1994 off-year election coverage along Voter Project lines.

Something important was starting. The decline in voter participation that expressed the American hatred of politics did not happen overnight and it will not be repaired overnight, but it was a beginning.

MOVING BEYOND ELECTIONS

Buoyed by our good feelings about the Voter Projects, the favorable anecdotal response to them, and the slight but positive movement in the public involvement needle, we decided to try to take the concept of dealing more directly with citizens beyond elections. That summer, with Managing Editor Smith again in charge, we developed a 10-week effort to address citizens' concerns about their lives. Starting with previous survey information and buttressed by structured interviews with almost 200 people, we focused on the issues of crime, education, government gridlock, and the fracturing of family life—issues of universal concern and frustration. Again, we recruited broadcast partners: KSNW Channel 3 and KNSS, a talk-radio station.

We called it "The People Project: Solving It Ourselves." The objective was to move beyond venting about the problems and involve people in thinking about solutions. Jon Roe was the lead writer. In the transient world of journalism, Roe is that rarest of creatures, but the sort that journalism must learn to cultivate and reward: He knows the community from a lifetime in it, possesses a high level of risk tolerance, and he cares. Several other reporters, artists, and photographers were also involved in the project that dominated the front page for more than 2 months.

Roe's lead stories spent little space describing the problems that everybody knew about, and even less space handwringing about them. Rather, they dealt with why no progress seems to be possible; with the core values that, unresolved, stand in the way of solution; and with the ideas of people who were trying to make some impression on the problem. His leads set up a package that included these departures from the newspaper norm:

- Success stories: Large and small examples of people who had made some difference, with emphasis on what motivated them to get involved.
- Core values graphics: Exercises that helped readers to sort out their core values and decide where they might be willing to consent to the existence of another view without compromising their own views.
- Advice on where to get involved: Exhaustive lists of organizations involved in seeking solutions in each of the areas of concern, sometimes nearly a full page of small type, with addresses and phone numbers. They were places where someone could help, or get help, and each ran several times.
- Notices of informal get-togethers sponsored by the broadcast partners and the newspaper: These were agendaless, unmoderated gatherings where people concerned about the problem could meet.
- Invitations to call, write, and fax ideas about solutions: Hundreds responded, and the freshest of the ideas appeared in print.

In November 1992, we published a two-week People Project on health care, a value-based approach that included a two-thirds page questionnaire designed to cause people to think about the trade-offs implicit in any health care reform. More than 5,000 people and families worked through the hour-long exercise, tore it out, put it in an envelope, stamped it, and sent it to us. It was an issue they cared deeply about and this was their chance, no matter how small, to get involved.

The result of all that effort? Nothing ... and everything. Circulation remained static. Revenues continued their slight decline. Kansas was not freed of crime or health care problems and the schools did not visibly improve—nor had we anticipated any of that. Yet thousands of people in south central Kansas spent time and energy in the second half of 1992 in an exercise in public life. Volunteerism in the Wichita school district was up 37% as the school year opened and, in an annual satisfaction survey, reader satisfaction with the *Eagle* rose an unprecedented 10 points—twice the increase among Knight–Ridder newspapers whose ratings rose at all.

It is important to note that the *Eagle* did not suspend traditional reporting efforts during those months. The agonizing struggle over abortion continued; a national election was held and covered; and stories of murders, rapes, tornadoes, and famine continued in the news. People began to see, however, that amid all that, their immediate concerns were being addressed by the newspaper and broadcast stations and their voices were being heard. They were back in the ballgame with us, and that was important to both of us.

In 1991 and 1992, others working in journalism and related fields were struggling with the same questions about the illness affecting public life. Most active among them was Jay Rosen at New York University, who was thinking and writing brilliantly from the academic's point of view. Among his associations was work with the Kettering Foundation of Dayton, Ohio, which had been trying for more than a decade to develop ways to improve deliberation in American public life.

Rosen and I first met at a seminar in New York City cosponsored by Kettering and the S.I. Newhouse School at Syracuse University. Rosen combined scholarly rigor with a drive to forge improvements in public life. The personal and professional chemistry between us overrode our strikingly dissimilar backgrounds—two decades in age; my Southern, small-town, purely journalism upbringing and training that had transferred to the plains of Kansas; his native-New Yorker, philosophy, academic background and training that stayed firmly planted in the midst of Manhattan.

Rosen's energy and the support of the Kettering Foundation persuaded The John S. and James L. Knight Foundation to fund The Project on Public Life and the Press, which became the leading force in support of new ways of looking at the journalistic mission. In a related area, the Pew Charitable Trust endowed the Center for Civic Journalism under Ed Fouhy, former network executive, with $4.5 million to help newspapers and broadcast stations develop experiments in the same field. By 1993, a burgeoning movement was underway, complete with strong dissenting voices, experimentation in many places, and the possibility of real change in a profession not accustomed to it.

PUBLIC LIFE CHANGES OUTSIDE JOURNALISM

The journalistic stirrings in Wichita and elsewhere were not occurring in isolation. The frustration that gripped much of the nation was simmering into action among concerned citizens. Many of these awakenings from malaise have been captured in Lappe and DuBois' (1994) *The Quickening of America*:

> From a workplace in Pittsburgh to senior housing in New York, from health clinics in Oregon to a youth organization in California, from barrios in Texas to a newspaper in Kansas, from a classroom in Florida to city hall in Seattle—all across America an invisible revolution is taking shape. There is one unmistakable common thread: ... it's dawning on more and more of us that the best decision making is shared. ... Across many arenas of American life, citizens are discovering that human beings grow into the most effective problem solvers when we ourselves "own" the challenge—when we participate in defining the problem and devising the solutions. (p. 72)

In one sense, that quickening philosophy is the antithesis of another powerful trend in American thought: personal growth and change through trying to perfect private relationships. As Lappe and DuBois (1994) pointed out:

> Best-selling self-help books coach us in finding ourselves through introspection ... and by working through issues of love and control in our intimate relationships. While many of these techniques can enhance our lives, they are simply not sufficient either to produce the individual happiness we want or the society we want. (p. 288)

By themselves, these techniques are not enough. However, one can argue that going through the private development phase, even though it is internalized, prepares the ground for the next step—turning that energy and insight into public purposes.

Whether the renewed interest in public problem solving is arrived at directly or indirectly through self-awareness, it is going on without much recognition by mainstream journalism. Why is that? Isn't it important for public life that journalists be attentive to such a promising trend? It is of course, but detachment and an oversimplified notion of fairness and balance, and a concern for appearing to be naive impose a stifling caution on journalists. For traditional journalists faced with such a trend as Lappe and DuBois (1994) reported on, all the limiting axioms come back into play. The conflicting concerns were starkly outlined in an exchange at a 1991 Kettering Foundation seminar involving journalists, academics, and foundation leaders, including myself and Howard Schneider, Managing Editor of Newsday:

Merritt: There were remarks made a while ago that we do a section on volunteering, but not in a celebrating way, and I guess I'm beginning to ask myself, in my declining years, why not do that in a celebrating way? Is there really anything controversial about people who volunteer in the community, and shouldn't we, in fact, celebrate that a little?

Schneider: I think that's the point. There can be things controversial about volunteering. Not all volunteer organizations are the same. ... When you start picking and choosing you're running into trouble.

Merritt: Why, if you pick the good ones and don't pick the bad ones?

Schneider: Because you are making a value judgment. You should report when they do good things and ... the way they spend their money. And when they don't spend their money in that way, you should report that, too. ... If the people who had poured money into Phoenix House had looked into [it] ... they might not have put all the money into Phoenix House.

Merritt: I understand that. But what I'm saying is that editors and reporters are supposed to be able to make those kinds of judgments, and some of it isn't easy.

Schneider: I think you're setting a horrible precedent with that attitude. United Way is very controversial in some communities. It's considered to be an organization that supports White establishment interests and not minority interests.

Merritt: Well, if you're going to do a volunteer section but in a noncelebrating way, are you going to put everybody in there and make no judgments?

Schneider: I wasn't planning to do the section. (Laughter) (pp. 92–95)

Cataloging what is going wrong is always safer than cataloging what is going right because wrong may be immediately demonstrable but right can always go wrong. Journalistic caution about validating success through treating it as important news limits citizens' knowledge of and discussion about the possibilities of public problem solving.

PART III

The Value of Values

As noted earlier (chapter 1), journalists are almost congenitally un-comfortable talking about values. The idea that dealing in values (other than the First Amendment, of course) and journalistic objectivity are professionally incompatible is an artifact of the canon of objectivity.

They are not incompatible, but our traditional aversion to dealing in values blinds us to the central fact that everyone else does. It is another of those trained incapacities created by the traditional jour-nalistic culture. The people whose trust we seek invariably, if some-times unconsciously, filter every idea they hear through their own value systems, forming an immediate bias as to the idea's validity: Is the idea in harmony with my personal experience and observations? Is it agreeable, or offensive, to my personal beliefs? Does it fit my moral framework? They give the idea credibility or not on the basis of that automatic calculation. Having formed that initial opinion, they have arrived at Yankelovich's (1991) first stage, raised consciousness.

Being willfully inattentive to that process, journalists expect people to be ready to decide about an issue simply because they have been informed about it. As noted in chapter 6, this impatient and unrealistic idea creates a disconnect. Before the public can reach resolution on an issue, it must "work through," in Yankelovich's terminology. This means, among other things, people recognizing that others might hold competing core values, and might process the ideas through a different set of experiences and beliefs. Reconciling those competing core values is the essence of working through to public judgment. Because it is a mandatory element in reaching resolution, it is futile for journalists to ignore it, yet we do ignore it because of our own uneasiness with discussions about values. While we go rushing off to raise conscious-ness on yet another matter, the issue is left unresolved and the public is left confused, frustrated, and cynical about our obvious hit-and-run tactics, which the public interprets as sensationalism and negative news.

Journalists need to develop the skill and vocabulary for dealing with values as they impinge on public issues, and not shrink from the necessary discussion and working through. It is a journalistic obligation to help the public recognize how personal core values affect their view of issues and how the failure to resolve competing core values stands in the way of effective deliberation aimed at solving problems.

THE FAIR-MINDED PARTICIPANT

As with values, journalists get jittery at any suggestion that they are, or should be, participants in anything except the detached practice of their arcane art. Detachment forbids participation. The media age reality, however, is that journalists become participants simply by being journalists. Whether we admit it or not, or are comfortable with the idea, the way we do our journalism has a direct impact on how public life goes. The very act of choosing to convey a fact or not convey it is an act of participation in public life. To deny this is to deny that our work has any meaning whatsoever. We do not launch stories out into a vacuum; they affect people and events. This reality imposes an obligation on journalists to consider the undeniable consequences of how they choose to tell the news.

If our traditional practices and culture have the effect of diminishing public life—a point that I believe is undeniable—then we must change our ways. This does not mean that we stop reporting legitimate news; it means that we report it in ways that can help public life go better. Public life "going better" does not mean smoothly or quietly, for that isn't the nature of a democracy of free-minded people. It means that people are engaged in public life; that democracy achieves its aims because the process works.

Because we are unavoidably participants and because our profession is dependent on democracy's continuing success, we need to develop a working philosophy of participation in helping public life go well. I call it *the fair-minded participant*.

Adopting that philosophy does not mean abandoning good judgment, fairness, balance, accuracy or truth. It does, however, mean employing those virtues on the field of play, not from the far-removed pressbox; not as a contestant, but as a fair-minded participant whose presence is necessary in order for outcomes to be determined fairly; that is, under the agreed-on rules, by the contestants.

Consider that sports analogy in the context of democratic decision making. The function of a third party—a referee or umpire or judge—in sports competition is to facilitate the deciding of the outcome, not to determine it. If things go according to the rules, he or she is neither seen nor heard. Yet the presence of a fair-minded participant is necessary in order for an equitable decision to be reached.

What he or she brings to the arena is knowledge of the agreed-on rules, the willingness to contribute that knowledge, and authority, which is the right to be attended to. The referee's role is to make sure that the process works as the contestants agreed it should. In order to maintain that authority, that right to be heard, the referee must exhibit no interest in the final outcome other than that it is arrived at under the rules. For both for referee and contestants, however, that is the ultimate interest.

Journalists should bring to the arena of public life knowledge of the rules—how the public has decided a democracy should work—and the ability and willingness to provide relevant information and a place for that information to be discussed and turned into democratic consent. Like the referee, to maintain our authority, our right to be heard, we must exhibit no partisan interest in the specific outcome other than that it is arrived at under the democratic process; not detached, but objective.

Of course sports contests can, and do, go on without referees, and in those games someone wins and someone loses: There is an outcome. However, the outcome is almost always determined on the basis of who is the loudest or strongest, who is most willing to hedge on the rules, who is willing to contest without resolution for the longest time, or who owns the ball. The same is true of public life. It can, and does, go on without journalists playing their appropriate role, but outcomes, if they occur, are decided on the same risky basis as the playground pick-up game. When critical public issues arise, something more substantial than playground pick-up rules is needed to increase the odds that the issues will be resolved at all and through the democratic process.

That's where the journalistic fair-minded participant becomes important. We act out of a value that "public life should go well."

The tradition that says journalists should not deal in the realm of values creates yet another disconnect between us (and our product) and citizens at large.

TWO CRITICAL DISJUNCTURES

The research of Neuman et al. (1992) demonstrates the disjuncture between journalistic practice and public reality where values are concerned:

> Regardless of the medium in which they work, journalists eschew the moral frame which figures prominently in the public's understanding of

issues. The public, [through the interviews] in contrast, relished and drew out the moral dimension in the human impact of issues, and underscored the moral dimensions of public policy. ...

The disjuncture in public and media frames demonstrates that alternative frames are out there in the public discourse on issues. In general, the journalists have shied away from the moral dimensions, remaining on the relatively safe ground of objectified news. Since some of these moral frames reinforce parochial and even bigoted values, it is not clear that the media's cautious avoidance of such perspectives serves best to enhance democratic competence.

Rather than hoping that news frames will overwhelm popular conceptions, the media could confront those conceptualizations head on and provide a range of challenging, alternative views. (pp. 112–113)

What this clearly means is that the public will continue to make up its mind in a framework that includes a values—moral—dimension, with or without our help. The longer it is done without the help of value-blind and risk-averse journalists, the less relevant we and our work become. Thus journalists need to develop both a new outlook (the fair-minded participant) and a new set of reporting skills that deal with the reality that values drive the world. We need to take the risk of applying both to our profession.

Some experiments have been tried, but many more are needed. In dealing with the issue of health-care reform in 1992, the *Wichita Eagle* invited readers to work through a core-values exercise on their own as a way to better understand the application of core values to a complex issue. Core values are the beliefs and priorities that lie beneath people's opinions. One example of competing core values about health care: that everyone of any age or medical status is entitled to every medical opportunity to live, on the one hand, and, on the other, that limited resources are better spent on people who can attain a reasonable quality of life.

We developed a graphic representation of some of the competing values that must be resolved in any health-care reform plan. Later, we experimented with similar exercises on other issues such as gun control and the death penalty. Encouraging people to discuss issues from the starting point of core values moves debate toward deliberation; in the Yankelovich (1991) model, it moves in reach of true public judgment.

No real deliberation exists, and no true resolution can occur, without core values being addressed. Until competing core values are acknowledged and subject to at least consent, the result is simply debate or discourse, the mere repetition of competing opinions.

BRIGHT SPOT IN AKRON

The art and the rewards of becoming the fair-minded participant and challenging citizens to address their core values were stunningly demonstrated in 1993 and early 1994 by the Akron *Beacon-Journal*.

Akron, Ohio, is a metropolitan area of 658,000 with a record of difficult race relations and economic hardships leading into the 1990s. As *Beacon-Journal* Editor Dale Allen (personal communication) wrote in March 1994:

> Like many newspapers, we learned from the Los Angeles riots that we didn't know as much about race relations as we thought we did.
>
> We decided it was time to look into the mirror of our own community, but to get deeper than the smoothly polished surface. In fact, 12 months of reporting showed an ugly reality that we knew would anger both blacks and whites. It did. But to get the message through without further polarizing the community, we adopted a novel approach, one that offered a glimmer of hope.

Rather than simply telling the news of Akron's racial tensions and sitting back to report on the reactions, Allen guided his newspaper into the center of the circumstances it was reporting on.

"A Question of Color," five multipart installments, were published over 11 months in 1993. The careful research and reporting behind the series bashed many racial stereotypes about such subjects as crime and education and business. Interracial focus groups convened by the newspaper discussed the implications of the information and possible solutions.

The newspaper then took a major step. The staff, as Allen wrote:

> went beyond consciousness raising—we made it possible for readers who wanted to be part of the solution to come together to set a community agenda.
>
> Reader coupons published with each series helped readers steer our reporters towards success stories in their communities. And scores of organizations volunteered to be part of future solutions.
>
> Assisted by 50 *Beacon-Journal* employees—journalists and nonjournalists from all parts of the building—who served as group moderators, these [200] citizens talked about the obstacles to improved race relations, then offered more than 100 ways to overcome them.

The *Beacon-Journal* published those ideas. It then asked citizens to make a New Year's resolution to "do everything I can to improve race relations in 1994" and to call, write, and fax the newspaper with their names. Is this a naive idea?

Stunningly, 22,000 Akron-area residents did respond (about 10% of the *Beacon-Journal's* Sunday circulation), and the newspaper published a special section listing every name. More significantly, the project continued into 1994, with more than 100 community groups meeting to plan projects with members of other groups of the opposite race.

Akron's racial problems are hardly solved, but the newspaper has moved the city out of the dregs of hopelessness, involved thousands of its citizens at some level of the problem, and helped develop a new capacity in the community, a new set of democratic skills that will serve the city well over the long term. As Allen pointed out, the newspaper neither set nor drove the agenda. It worked as a catalyst, that is it provided the shared information and the agora, so that citizens could not only feel empowered to make progress but could actually experience progress.

The Akron project could not have happened unless Allen and the other journalists on his staff had been willing to move beyond studied detachment and recognize their personal and professional stakes in the public life of the community. They acted on an important value: that race relations in their city should be better. That is how the fair-minded participant operates effectively and begins to repair the three disconnections between journalists and citizens, in the public, and between the public and institutions such as government.

THE ABORTION EXAMPLE

Another example of how values play strongly, if in some ways negatively, in public life can be seen in the debate over abortion, a hard-rock issue steeped in religious and moral beliefs and clearly confiscated by absolutists on each side. Although every survey shows that the great majority of Americans are in neither absolutist camp, the way in which the issue is consistently framed by politicians and journalists blinds the participants and the public at large to possible bargainable points.

In January of 1997, as in each preceding year, journalists dutifully reported on the "two sides" of the abortion question gathering in Washington and various state capitals to stake their claims to rectitude. The two sides represented at the demonstrations hardly reflected America. Of all the issues that divide us, abortion has more sides, more permutations of differing beliefs, than almost any other. So the great majority of Americans, almost 70% of whom are in neither camp according to reliable surveys, did not participate in person or in their hearts and minds. As a result, the demonstrations amounted to simply another skirmish in a long and bitter war among minority believers.

The demonstrations were a manifestation of our decades-long debate over rights, legal and moral. Does a woman have a legal right to determine what happens to her own body? Does an unborn child have a legal right to be born? Are those rights absolute in either case? The absence or existence of a legal right is certainly worth debating in a democracy, and the current state of the law in this democracy is that a woman does have a right, under certain conditions, to decide to have abortion. Abortion opponents want to change that law; people who believe a woman has a right to decide want to keep it.

The objective of arguing over legal rights is to prevail, to get one's way about how those rights are defined; that is not the same thing as resolving the underlying problems created by the existence or absence of the legal right. Whichever side prevails at any given time in the legal argument over abortion, two things, at least, are certain:

- The issue of moral right will not be resolved; morality is, by definition, a matter of individual conscience that occasionally, but not often, resolves itself into a societal morality.
- The perceived need for and actual use of abortions will not disappear.

The core question that democracy seeks to answer through consent, not through legal or moral coercion, is "What shall we do?" It is a pragmatic question, not a question of defining rights. It is the practical matter of deciding what people in a democracy are going to do about a situation. Bear in mind, the question democracy seeks to answer is not "What shall we think, or believe?" It's "What shall we do?" Democracy does not contemplate that people need to think and believe in the same way, even about democracy itself; in fact, democracy is built on the idea that people of differing beliefs can find a way to resolve problems and live together in peace.

No one argues that abortions are good. Given such agreement on a fundamental value, why cannot the nation find ways to make abortions a thing of the past? Could it have to do with the way the issue is framed and presented by activists and journalists? What if the thrust of coverage of the abortion issue were on the value that virtually all Americans agree on rather than on the values that separate them? This does not mean ignoring the divisions, for they are news by any definition; it is a matter of emphasis. What except habit, tradition, and a thirst for conflict stops journalists from deciding that broad agreement on a fundamental issue is important news?

Unless we develop the skills and language to understand and report about how the public process actually works, what we reflect back to readers and viewers can and will be dismissed as mere spectacle, something to be, at best, observed, such as the annual Roe *v* Wade demonstrations.

Avoiding spectacle means dealing not just with absolutes, but also with the reasonable possibilities of useful compromise. Because the majority of Americans are ambivalent to some degree on the issue of abortion, they do not see themselves reflected in the bipolar, absolutist arguments; they turn away from the issue as unresolvable. Thus, while the absolutists argue from their entrenched positions, unwanted and crisis pregnancies continue to rise and adoption processes and laws remain archaic so the number of abortions continues to rise. Purposeful reporting that minimizes spectacle, explores the core values at stake beyond simply "no" and "yes," and deals with the possibilities of useful compromise can help create the sort of deliberation that leads to resolution, even of so profound an issue.

❖ N I N E ❖

The Value of Deliberation

> *So the printers can never leave us in a state of perfect rest
> and union of opinion. They would be no longer useful, and would
> have to go to the plow.*
>
> —Thomas Jefferson[1]

Jefferson's wry comment contrasted with his more famous (and far more often quoted by journalists) declaration about choosing newspapers without government over government without newspapers, and the two reflected a soundly based ambivalence over the effect of journalism that continues today.

Journalism does have a superficial and beguiling stake in foment and agitation; that is the stuff of "great stories" and is thought by journalists to be of primary interest to the public; it sells newspapers and hypes ratings, the theory contends. Foment and agitation are also a sign and inevitable product of a healthy democracy. When, however, foment and agitation are the end product rather than a means to an end, issues are perpetuated rather than resolved, bogging down democracy and creating hopelessness and cynicism.

Journalism has an even larger, if less obvious and entertaining, stake in issues being resolved rather than having them stew in agitation. When issues are resolved, when hopelessness and cynicism are replaced by hope and optimism, people are encouraged to become engaged in attacking the next issue. People engaged in public life, many studies have shown, are avid consumers of the journalistic product.

The way issues are resolved in a democracy is through some version of deliberation, formal or informal, a point well demonstrated by Yankelovich's (1991) studies. So journalists would do well, for themselves and public life, to understand the process of deliberation and encourage it in the way we report on issues.

---

[1]Jefferson letter to Elbridge Gerry, March 29, 1801.

Mathews, in *Politics for People*, (1994) explains deliberation in this way:

> To deliberate is not just to "talk about" problems. To deliberate means to weigh carefully both the consequences of various options for action and the views of others. Deliberation is what we require of juries. It is what makes twelve of our peers a group to whom we literally give life-or-death powers. We don't just trust twelve people with those powers under any conditions. We require that they deliberate long and carefully. The same is true of democratic politics. Without the discipline of serious deliberation, it is impossible for a body of people to articulate what they believe to be in the best interest of all—in the "public" interest. Deliberations are needed to find our broader and common concerns ... without deliberation, governments are left without public direction and legitimacy. (p. 111)

Deliberation, as Mathews and others pointed out, does not guarantee that anything will happen, but it "creates the possibility that an action will be taken mindful of the consequences. Deliberation helps us look before we leap" (p. 182).

Briand (1994), writing for the Project on Public Life and the Press, explained:

> A public that lacks a shared perspective on a problem is no more able to carry out the essential political task—that of forming a sound judgment and making a choice—than a person with multiple personalities would be able to act rationally if all his various "selves" were present simultaneously and were clamoring for the right to motivate his actions.
> ...
>
> A public judgment consists of a shared sense of which consequences are acceptable to everyone, which are not, what trade-offs people are prepared to accept, and what priorities we should have as a public. (pp. 5–6)

Public judgment arrived at through deliberation:

> [is not] simple compromise—the negotiated giving up of something in order to obtain a reciprocal concession. Rather, [it] represents a shared conclusion about what is best, all things considered and in the circumstance for everyone. A public judgment never loses sight of the importance of the good things that might have to be assigned relatively less emphasis in order to resolve a conflict. Accordingly, it insists that they be respected insofar as is possible.
>
> In practice, a public judgment is achieved when people reach the threshold of agreement expressed in phrases such as "what we can all live with" or what everyone can get along with. (pp. 6–7)

In other words, public judgment is consent, not consensus.

Hunter (1994), in *Before The Shooting Begins*, provided an insightful, and hopeful, exploration of the possibilities for consent—as opposed to consensus—in the value-laden, morality driven cultural war over abortion. The priority for a democracy facing such a gut issue, he wrote:

> Is to find not the "middle ground" of fast moral compromise but rather a "common ground" where the particularities of people's beliefs are indeed recognized as sacred to the people who hold them (and, therefore, as nonnegotiable), but common problems can nevertheless be addressed.

That common ground, he stressed:

> is not "dialogue" in the vacuous sense often invoked by some ministers, marriage counselors and conflict-resolution specialists. It is, rather, robust and passionate and utterly serious civil reflection and argument. … [It is] a public agreement about how to disagree publicly. … Only in this context can there exist the possibility of forging politically sustainable solutions to the conflicts that divide us.

> In the final analysis, substantive argument is the one essential ingredient that can make the concept of democracy—and the consent it implies—meaningful. … [however] … it is by its nature a long-term and messy proposition, particularly when the cleavages in the nation become deep. (p. 35)

Hunter and Briand are very close to prescribing for this century what happened in the ancient agora, and they precisely pinpoint what needs to happen in the modern agora that journalism can provide. In doing so, they raise a difficult and direct challenge for journalists, for if we do not foster, inform, and support that long-term, messy, robust, passionate, and utterly serious civil reflection and argument, it will not occur, and any chance for consent will be lost.

AN UNNATURAL ACT?

In today's information age, public deliberation rarely occurs naturally. We are bombarded with information and what passes for information from all sides at every moment. The mediums providing most of this information—print, broadcast, the Internet—are geared to transience; their perceived need for immediacy and freshness overwhelms any opportunity for contemplation except by the most withdrawn and determined. Living in that deluge has acclimated an entire generation of Americans to that same transience of attention and thought. We hardly assimilate one matter or set of facts when another comes crashing upon us. Our false perception is that because a matter is gone from immediate attention, it must no longer be important or has been resolved. Actually, it has only been shoved aside by some new awareness.

Nowhere is this more sharply seen than in television, whose culture is one of instantaneous change and whose purveyors of news feel compelled to devote no more than 90 seconds to most subjects, no matter how complex or serious.

This is true even on ostensible discussion shows, which could provide some opportunity for deliberation but dissolve into argumentation, the objective of which is to prevail rather than to resolve. People sitting around deliberating is thought to make dull television, so the examples of discussion that people see, even among our most notable figures, is a travesty of thoughtfulness.

Following are excerpts from the transcript of a "discussion" on an important issue: U.S. policy in 1994 toward Haiti.

The principals are two U.S. Senators, members of the "world's greatest deliberative body," John McCain of Arizona and Bob Graham of Florida, and the show's cohosts, John Sununu and Juan Williams. As you read it, imagine yourself as a citizen potentially interested in the pros and cons of the issue and seeking some ground on which to base an opinion:

Graham:	John, first, I have been to Haiti a number of times, as recently as within the last three weeks. The people of Haiti are—
McCain:	I thought you were turned away.
Graham:	I was—I have been declared persona non grata. I can't go back.
Sununu:	There or here?
Graham:	And the people of Haiti are anxious for the return of President Aristide because they understand—
McCain:	Are they anxious for a U.S. invasion?
Graham:	—there is not going to be any beginning of a process of rejoining the community of nations, of any economic assistance, of political legitimacy until—
McCain:	But, Bob, are they eager for a U.S. invasion?
Graham:	Yes, they are eager for a U.S. invasion—
McCain:	I don't believe that.
Graham:	—because they are the ones who are being slaughtered in the streets. They are the ones who are the objects of those horrendous human rights abuses that Juan just outlined.

McCain:	I don't believe that. Many of them remember our previous 19-year occupation and no one believes that Haiti was better off for the experience.
Graham:	John, you keep talking about that previous occupation of—
McCain:	Look, if you ignore the lessons of history, my friend, you will repeat them.
Graham:	John, there is no—
McCain:	If you ignore those lessons, you are going to repeat them, and when you invade militarily—
Graham:	There is no necessity for the United States to repeat the lessons of what—
McCain:	Well, why don't you get Aristide to say he wants an invasion, if you think it's such a wonderful option? Why don't you get President Aristide to say he wants an invasion? Then I think you would have more viability to your argument.
Williams:	All right, gentlemen, let's take a break.

(Later in the show)

McCain:	The important thing is, how many American lives do you want to risk, recess or not, Bob? How many do you want to risk?
Sununu:	Senator McCain—
McCain:	Fifty, 100, 200?
Graham:	I do not believe—
McCain:	And the aftermath—

| Sununu: | We're going to have to cut if off here, gentlemen. ... Juan and I will be back in a second |

(After a commercial break, Williams and Sununu set out to conclude the discussion.)

Sununu:	Juan, I'm glad to see you're supporting President Clinton's policy. Now, does that mean you supported the flips and the flops and whatever flips and flops follow this?
Williams:	Unbelievable, Mr. Sununu. Here you are as a Bush administration man—
Sununu:	We were at least consistent. This is a guy that has gone back and forth—
Williams:	Yeah, you were consistent. Did nothing.
Sununu:	—back and forth.

Williams:	You did absolutely nothing—
Sununu:	What we did is at least keep the boat people from drowning, and what we did is have credibility—
Williams:	Yeah, you kept people—
Sununu:	—that when George Bush said we're going to use force, people believed it.
Williams:	You let people live under a repressive political situation. You did nothing to do it—and now this honest man tries to—
Sununu:	This honest man???
Williams:	—resolve it, and Bill Clinton gets nothing but your—
Sununu:	He can't make up his mind. He can't make up his mind whether he's in favor of force, against force—
Williams:	Stop it, John.
Sununu:	No credibility and no capacity—
Williams:	These people don't believe you ...
Sununu:	—to do anything worthwhile.

These are two U.S. senators and two journalism stars engaged in political discourse. Why do Americans hate politics?

As Dionne (1992) pointed out, debate on issues is carried out by liberals and conservatives in a framework of false choices mired in ideology. The core values that constitute the ideology rarely surface and certainly are never seen as subject to deliberation and consent. Because that false method of discourse is embedded in our professional politics at the highest level, it is mirrored in political debate at all levels. It migrates from the halls of Congress to the town hall to the talk radio show to the barber shop, and its method of migration is, of course, journalism.

RECOGNIZING DELIBERATION: SOME EXAMPLES

Deliberation—so natural a process when we face individual decisions about our lives such as what career to pursue, which new car to purchase, whether to marry—is for groups of strangers a learned civic skill. It has been part of human cultures over the centuries, as in the Roman forum, in American colonial town meetings, and, in many nations, the gatherings of tribal chiefs. Some observers believe there is a human instinct for deliberation, but its presence or absence is often a function of the immediate culture.

Page and Shapiro, who studied public attitudes over 50 years, find contemporary American culture not conducive to public deliberation. In *The Rational Public*, they wrote:

In a country where only about half the eligible citizens vote in presidential elections, where town meetings are rare, where most work places are hierarchical, and where most citizens are not mobilized by a congenial issue-oriented party or political group, the educational potential of participation is not fully realized.

They might have added to the impediments a media culture in which deliberation is not valued and its potential is not understood.

Can journalism be a factor in developing citizens' civic skills, particularly deliberation, without damage to its news-giving function? I believe the answer is "yes," but it will require of journalists a deeper understanding of the dynamics of deliberation and the role it can play in a healthy public life.[2]

A dramatic demonstration of how deliberation can turn simple opinion into more thoughtful judgment occurred at the University of Texas in 1996. The National Issues Convention brought 459 randomly selected Americans to Austin to discuss an array of issues such as foreign aid, education, welfare, and family pressures. The delegates included business people, teachers, a rock band member or two, welfare mothers, students—the range of America's population. The only commonality among the delegates was their willingness to spend the weekend (not at their own expense) and to respond to two lengthy surveys, one before and one after the sessions.

The surveys asked their opinions on a broad range of issues, many of which they discussed during the weekend in groups of about 20, aided by trained moderators. They were provided, after the first survey but before the sessions, factual background material on the issues that a bipartisan committee of former government officials and office-holders agreed was objective and complete. The discussion often became intense as delegates' preconceptions collided with the facts and with the opposite opinions of others around the circles. Tightly held values underlying their opinions faced bold challenges from people with opposite core values; assumptions about events and people were tested, sometimes severely.

After the 3 days of discussion, they retook the survey. On many critical issues, their opinions changed although their core values did not. Faced with shared, relevant information and a place in which to discuss its implications with other citizens, they were much closer to agreement on many issues, dramatically so in some cases. Where they wound up on specific issues is much less important for our purposes than the fact that the process moved them from mere opinion to a more thoughtful and common judgment.

---

[2]A number of groups and foundations are active in promoting deliberation, notable The Kettering Foundation through the National Issues Forum, Public Agenda and The National Civic League.

Although the Austin experiment involved expensive and complex arrangements, encouraging deliberative skills through journalism is not necessarily a matter of bringing people together for formal sessions, although some newspapers and broadcast outlets have done that as part of public journalism projects. For journalists who may be squeamish about so active a role or for those without the resources, the potential—as with much of public journalism practice—lies in the way we approach daily and weekly stories. And, as with much of public journalism practice, doing it requires attention and patience, an understanding of deliberation, and the belief that building civic capital is a fundamental part of the journalistic role.

Here is one simple example of day-to-day reporting that advances better understanding of an issue. Wichita was embroiled in an angry debate over a local handgun-control ordinance. The City Council held a public hearing and several hundred people jammed into the council chambers. Over almost 9 hours, more than 100 people expressed strong pro and con opinions, trying to persuade the council. Public hearings are not deliberation; they are argumentation aimed at prevailing. Our reporter, however, heard more than the emotional pleas of absolutists on each side. He also heard people expressing ambivalence; people who felt strongly about individual rights but who were struggling with the societal implications of no controls at all on handguns; citizens with stories to tell of their personal struggle with the issue.

Traditional reports of that hearing would have highlighted the considerable emotional content from both sides, using first the most explosive quote from the pros and balancing it with the most explosive quote from the cons, and so on down the descending scale of conflict. That would have made a good story and would have framed the issue in stark contrasts. Our story, however, went deeper. Key paragraphs well up in the story added the element of ambivalence and framed the issue in all its complexity rather than merely at the extremes. It said, in effect, this is a difficult issue for many people, not a simply "for" or "against" matter, and many people are struggling over it.

This approach had at least three important virtues:

- Primarily, of course, it was more accurate than merely reporting the polar opposites.
- It allowed readers who were not in the chamber to understand the issue in a richer way.
- It allowed citizens who harbored some ambivalence to understand that their views, too, were important and a part of the discussion. They were not excluded by the reporter's framing.

It was only one story on one day, so its effect was not directly measurable; but it avoided two traps: the trap of framing the issue too narrowly through oversimplified conflict (while recognizing the truly deep conflicts); and the trap of episodic superficiality. Was it "just good journalism?" One could make that theoretical argument, but the fact is that 3 years previously, we would not have written the story that way and few other newspapers would do it that way today.

Public learning about deliberation and resolving conflict is a long and complex process not accomplished with one incident or one story but over time through accumulated experiences.

That fact illuminates another way in which journalists can help engage people in public life: treating it as news when they do, even if it is occurring on what seems to be a minor level. In 1993, Wichita had only a handful of active neighborhood associations, organizations in which people in a geographic area come together to resolve common problems, whether the problem is crime, a zoning matter, or the need to clean up the neighborhood. We began to treat what those associations were doing as news, as demonstrations of what people taking personal responsibility can do to improve their lives. In 1997, there were almost 60 such groups. Other factors, including an umbrella neighborhood association, were at work, and the newspaper was not involved in organizing anything. However, as people in the community learned through the newspaper of the work of others, they became encouraged and hopeful about their own roles and learned the value of deliberation. This was simply a matter of broadening our definition of news to include the work people were doing that mattered a great deal in their personal lives. They became engaged in public life.

Something to Think About

Building civic capital, such as deliberative skills, is not traditionally considered to be a journalistic function. The inescapable fact, however, is that the way we do journalism has a strong effect on how people see themselves and their environment. If people see themselves as having no effective role in public life, as barred by circumstance from any control over their lives, they will continue to withdraw and democracy will be weakened.

❖ T E N ❖

So Far, so Good ... Mostly

> *If this is important change, if it's really fundamental and you've been at it only 3 or 4 years and think you're seeing progress, then you're not asking all the right questions and you're not looking in all the right places.*
> —Balbir Mathus (personal communication, December 1994)

My friend Balbir Mathur's cautionary words (see Preface) are now 3 years old as this is written, making it almost 7 years that a group of journalists and academics have been thinking, writing, and debating about the idea of public journalism. In that time, the roster of journalists experimenting with the philosophy has grown from a handful to thousands and the number of newspapers involved at some level from three or four in the United States to several hundred on five continents. We are trying to look in all the right places and ask all the right questions so that the public journalism philosophy is submitted to the most rigorous tests of practicality.

Experimenting is the operative word. From its inception, public journalism has been an idea seeking meaningful application rather than a set of operational principles or set of rules. People unwilling to make the intellectual journey to understand it are destined to do public journalism badly, and in fact have done it badly.

The reality of its experimental nature, as much as any one factor, made public journalism immediately controversial within the profession. That's because:

- Journalists tend toward pragmatism. As one critic put it, "Don't those (public journalism) people know that journalists are 'how to' people?"
- The unavoidable absence of a brief, immediately understandable, one-paragraph definition invites critics to craft their own strawmen definitions and immediately set them ablaze, which dozens have done.

112

- Our profession, in fact our society as a whole, demands instant, measurable results from any proposed change. Public journalism, by its very nature, is long-term cultural change. The accepted practices of today did not spring full blown, they evolved. Changing the culture of a mature profession will take time, as will improving the nature of public life.
- It is not yet clear how deeply traditional practices will be affected, thus many critics wrongly assume that public journalism seeks to replace every journalistic tradition. It does not; it is additive, contending that much of the traditional practice is not wrong so much as it is insufficient in today's environment.
- Public journalism suggests that some of the practices that have moved people to the top of the profession, the elite newspapers and networks, might not have been altogether appropriate and best for public life or journalism. This offends and somehow seems to threaten those high achievers, who have been virtually unanimous in their condemnation, if not their efforts to understand. The unavoidable and gaping differences between those elite newspapers and the rest of the profession are dealt with elsewhere, but the question arises of whether those journalists are the ones who should define "good journalism" for all places and times (see The Dangers of Transience, chapter 4).

PUBLIC JOURNALISM HAS JOURNALISM DONE TO IT

If you talk about the foundation of public journalism for 15 minutes or so to a group of nonjournalists interested in public life, heads begin to nod affirmatively; the reaction is, "Of course, that's what journalism ought to be about. Why isn't it?" They get it. The same is true with most foreign journalists, particularly in nations where democracy is only now emerging, such as Latin America and Eastern Europe. Those professionals understand and appreciate the dynamic between journalism and democracy because they have experienced firsthand both its absence and its affirming emergence. The puzzlement, objections, and outright dismissal of the idea arise only in U.S. journalists, who for the most part seem either uninterested in or fearful of even discussing fundamental change, much less implementing it.

As a result of that difference, commentary on the idea during its first few years has been largely positive in foreign journals and the literature of civic activists, and largely negative in U.S. newspapers and journals.

In a broad sense, one can interpret the consistent differences in reaction as a symptom of the disconnect of most American journalists from the rest of the world, as yet another artifact of the ritual of determined detachment. In a more narrow, and barely more charitable, sense one can attribute the negative journalistic reaction to a failure to actually engage the idea itself.

At times, that failure to engage has been willful. In mid-1995, Max Frankel, former editor of *The New York Times*, decided to write a column about public journalism. He called me and asked, "What is your agenda for the city of Wichita?"

"I have no agenda," I responded.

"But in public journalism, the newspaper sets the agenda for the community, doesn't it?"

"No, I don't know what you mean."

His next few questions indicated that his misperceptions were based on one early experiment that was labelled as public journalism and on an underresearched article in one journal.

"Look," I finally said, "if you want to know what I think public journalism is about, I've just published a book; it's short, 130 pages or so, and you can read it in a couple of hours. It's published just across the river in New Jersey and I'll have a copy on your desk in the morning."

"No, thank you," he replied crisply, and his column on the *Times* op ed page was both dismissive of and misinformed about the idea.

Such events, and there have been dozens, have led me to note, sorrowfully, that "public journalism has had journalism done to it." When I say that to groups of non-journalists, they chuckle and nod in apparent understanding; when I say that to a group of journalists, they simply blink.

The tragic fact is that the way most journalists have treated the idea is a telling catalogue of what ails my profession: superficial reporting, the reliance on secondary and tertiary rather than primary sources; emphasis on the conflict over ideas as opposed to ideas themselves; adversarialism as opposed to healthy skepticism, which is to say setting out to oppose ideas rather than submitting them to rigorous questioning; framing false choices: if public journalism is not A then it must be Z; outright purblindness, a trained incapacity or a willful refusal to see the broad context of facts and events; the feeding frenzy, a specific example of which follows.

These peculiar, if predictable, reactions were seen not only in professional journals but also were heard in dozens of seminars and panel discussions. Often, it seemed that the pros and the cons could not have been discussing the same subject, so foreign were their impressions and opinions.[1]

---

[1]For a thorough, balanced critique of public journalism by a nonparticipant, see "*Civic Journalism,*"*CQ Researcher, Vol. 6,* No. 35, pp. 817–840, Sept. 20, 1996.

An entire separate volume could be written analyzing how and why public journalism had journalism done to it, and perhaps someone will do so. It would be a heart-rending and chastening experience for someone who loves the profession, so I will leave that dreary task to others and deal in detail with only one example.

NORTH CAROLINA ELECTION, 1996

Some of the clearest manifestations of public journalism ideas have occurred in election coverage. It is there, after all, where public life is most directly played out, and it is the hijacking of the electoral process by special interests that most frustrates Americans and renders them cynical about public life.

To attack that problem, newspapers working with public journalism make an important distinction between the election and the campaign. They see the campaign as what the candidates and handlers do and the election—the making of a choice—as what citizens do, and shift their emphasis away from detailing the machinations of the campaign and onto helping citizens with the important task they face. This does not mean that the campaign is ignored, but more of the staff's resources are devoted to the election.

In the fall of 1996, *The Charlotte Observer* and a number of other North Carolina newspapers agreed to pool some of their coverage efforts, which allowed them to share basic material about candidates' stands on issues. The arrangement allowed each newspaper to give its readers more and better information than it could have alone. It can be argued that such an arrangement is risky for newspapers because it plays into the hands of people who believe that newspapers are just one big leftist cabal; but the shared material amounted to only about 20% of the election material printed, so their natural competition on the other 80% was unaffected.

Within 3weeks, *The Washington Post*, *The New York Times*, *The Boston Globe* and *New Yorker* magazine each ran scathing critiques of the N.C. coverage. The pieces were unvaryingly conclusory and condemning of what the writers felt was journalistic tampering with election campaigns. They were virtually sputtering in their anxiety to condemn the coalition's effort to help voters make an informed decision. At the heart of their concern—at least as expressed in the stories—was the fact that the coalition had (gasp!) asked voters what issues *the voters* wanted the candidates to address, then pushed the candidates to address those issues. The inclusion of voters' voices in the campaign coverage was branded, variously in the critical articles, as fraud, manipulative, and dishonest.

It is difficult to understand how asking voters what they want the candidates to talk about can approach anything like fraud until one recognizes what a threat such unleashed populism presents to the elite political press.

That journalistic gentry believes it is supposed to tell citizens what issues to be concerned about, not the other way around; reversing the flow is akin to a threat of emasculation. Further, it threatens the cozy, incestuous relationship between the political journalists and the politicians they cover, a relationship that has allowed political campaigning to degenerate into a meaningless minuet of tactics, superficiality, and insider trading in ego gratification.

The four pieces were strikingly similar. In each, the reporters were attracted by a key U.S. Senate race, a repeat of 1990 with Democrat Harvey Gantt challenging long-time incumbent Sen. Jesse Helms, a Republican. What effect, they ostensibly wanted to know and report, was the coalition coverage having on that race? So what did they do to report this story of some newspapers' efforts to engage citizens in the election? They rushed off to North Carolina and interviewed the candidates and their handlers. Not surprisingly, they found the candidates and their handlers deeply unhappy about no longer being in full control of the electoral dialogue. The reporters also talked to a few journalists involved but only to demand that they respond to the campaigns' protests.

Here's the telltale point: Nowhere in any of those reports did the writers reflect a single conversation with a citizen to find out if the citizens of North Carolina were benefiting from the information they were getting. It is, after all, citizens who are the largest stakeholders in an election, not the candidates or the journalists.

Had the reporters talked to affected citizens before reaching their conclusions, they would have discovered at least some of the following: Of N.C. registered voters aware of the coalition's efforts (one fourth, or 1 million voters, were), a third felt that they were better informed than in previous elections; 8 in 10 viewed the effort favorably; and a majority of them said they based their vote on the candidates' stands on the issues.[2]

That reportorial failure clearly demonstrates a deep-seated and dangerous belief that elections are the property of politicians and journalists and not of the public; that citizens are supposed to be mere spectators during political campaigns that are conceived, formed, and carried out by political insiders with the score being kept and periodically announced by insider journalists.

The pieces, as a body, reflected each of the ailments just listed: superficial reporting, the reliance on secondary and tertiary rather

---

[2] "Your Voice, Your Vote," survey of registered voters in North Carolina, November 1996, by Frederick Schneiders Research, Washington, DC.

than primary sources; emphasis on the conflict over ideas as opposed to ideas themselves; adversarialism as opposed to healthy skepticism, which is to say setting out to oppose ideas rather than submitting them to rigorous questioning; framing false choices: if public journalism is not A then it must be Z; outright purblindness, a trained incapacity or a willful refusal to see the broad context of facts and events; and the feeding frenzy.

AVOIDING ONE JOURNALISM

The foregoing should not be seen as dismissive of all criticism and critics. Many experiments in public journalism went too far, in my view and deserve being labelled "advocacy," "meddling," or "marketing"; some have clearly been designed only to provide a short-term, high-profile impact on a problem, which can only add to the public's store of cynicism when the problem does not disappear.

When publishers and editors—and, by inference, their staffs—become actively involved in organizing specific solutions, they move beyond what I feel is appropriate and protective of our role as fair-minded participant in public life.

Other experiments have involved organizing community discussions, both episodic and continuing; inviting citizens to become involved in the decision-making process of the newspaper or broadcast outlet; actively promoting citizen involvement in such problems as race relations and crime, or covering elections and other political issues in more activist ways. The experiments offer an array of ideas that break out of the traditional mold. By my lights, some of those experiments fall on acceptable middle ground, some do not. But that is my middle ground, not everyone's.

With many critics of public journalism, there is no middle ground. Observing some experiments that by almost anyone's measure go too far, they condemn the entire idea. Recall that in 1993, NBC faked the blowing-up of a pickup truck as part of an investigative report on the dangers of side gas tanks. The journalistic profession was properly condemning of the network's excess, but no voices were heard condemning the entire idea of investigative journalism simply because someone did something stupid.

The concept of middle ground is important. Journalists traditionally talk about "the line" and some event or coverage as crossing the line as if there were one line, with everything on one side of it being good journalism and everything on the other side being something else. The formulation assumes that all important journalistic points—fairness, ethical behavior, proper detachment/attachment—fall neatly along that single line, "the line," and that everyone in the profession understands where it is and sees it the same way.

A more useful—and realistic—formulation considers two lines that define a continuum. At one edge, say the left side, is the traditional idea of total detachment. At the other, the right side, is total involvement and extreme political manipulation. Adopting the continuum model immediately changes the philosophical environment. Suddenly more possibilities exist for making journalistically proper connections, for the two lines define some middle ground. Journalists who venture into that new ground will have to decide, over time, whether their institutions and their communities are best served by that movement.

Venturing into that ground, however, can involve several levels of risk for journalists, not the least of which is career risk. Most of the nation's elite newspapers (I use the term in its narrow, not its pejorative sense) have not, as yet, found public journalism a viable idea. For reasons whose validly is open to question, it is those newspapers that remain the arbiters and definers of good journalism.

One reason is immediately understandable. They control what are historically seen as the best jobs, the top of the profession where reside fame, power, and, increasingly and perversely, the possibility of substantial wealth from television appearances, books, speaking fees, and other sidelines.

Another reason they maintain their preeminence as models in the profession is less understandable. The elite newspapers—*The Washington Post, The New York Times, The Wall Street Journal, The Los Angeles Times*—are separate from the rest of the profession because they serve elite, national audiences. Leaders at all levels and in all professions will read them if for no other reason than that they must. The journalism that they do is targeted, specific, and often excellent, but it is only one kind of journalism aimed at a narrow but amorphous national community of leaders. Their emphases, processes, interests, standards, and ethics are not necessarily the most appropriate ones for all of journalism.[3] Yet their status as models for all of journalism in every place persists, discouraging innovation other than their own and reinforcing the status quo as defined by them.

This notion of One Journalism no longer, if it ever did, well serves the rest of the profession and public life. If the problems and culture of Washington and New York and Wichita and Spokane were identical, an identical journalistic approach to them could work. They are not

---

[3]At a seminar at Harvard in 1994, a questioner asked Leonard Downie, editor of *The Washington Post*, if, because his newspaper operated in what was arguably the nation's worst city for crime and poverty, he felt any responsibility for doing something about it. His complete answer, "No."

identical, and the differences in people, history, politics, and ambitions mandate that journalists in each place develop not only specific practical approaches to their tasks but also remain flexible in their philosophical approaches.

Steven Smith, (1997) now editor of the *Colorado Springs Gazette Telegraph*, dealt with the dual issues of public journalism critics and One Journalism thinking this way in a talk to a workshop of people interested in public journalism:

> From where I sit, it seems as if public journalism is being victimized by the media elite. It is striking to me ... that there is so much less (critical) debate over civic journalism in the South, the Midwest (the crucible of public journalism) and even the Far West.
>
> But the big guns from Washington, New York and Boston—and the big gun wannabes—are the folks who have targeted journalists like me, and like you. Yet they are the journalists removed from newspapers like mine, from communities like mine.
>
> They don't read my paper. They never before concerned themselves with my journalistic values or practices. They don't know or care about the problems facing my community. Or yours. And I don't expect them to.
>
> I don't know how to define (public) journalism for a national newspaper. ... As far as I am concerned, how or even whether these concepts are embraced by the *Times*, *Journal* or *Post* editors is their affair.
>
> But I do care how (public) journalism is defined, defended and, ultimately, embraced by editors of community papers like my own. (p. 3)

Moving into that uncharted ground beyond traditional practices involves additional risks: of being misunderstood by either the public or peers; of facing choices that have no comforting precedents; and, of course, of error. Those risks can be mitigated in two ways. First, by venturing into that ground only after developing a fine sense of purpose and understanding how that purpose can serve both journalism and public life. The second is by being public about what you are doing, explaining in clear terms to those affected what your objectives are and the reasons behind those objectives. That's another reason why it's called public journalism.

The challenge is to change the newsroom culture from one that values detachment to one that values proper attachment, but any step, small or large, beyond calculated detachment is encouraging if only because it begins to dismantle the idea of One Journalism. The concept that there is and must be one homologous way of thinking and acting guided by immutable and arcane rules smacks of a priesthood, a status comforting to its introverted initiates but forbidding and unpersuasive to citizen outsiders.

Those who require the validation of the high priests of One Journalism might be disconcerted and deterred by the priesthood's disapproval. Certainly journalism's historic slow pace of change indicates that to be the case. Those recognizing the need for fundamental change and venturing down the road of public journalism, however, do not need such validation. Their experiences as their communities begin to approach public life with renewed vigor will be validation enough.

❖ E L E V E N ❖

Some Tools and Their Uses

If the goal of public journalism is to help public life go well by engaging people in it, how can that be accomplished? What tools and techniques can be brought to the task?

I approach the practical side with considerable reluctance based on frustrating experiences over the past several years. Because it is experimental, public journalism has no handy, one-sentence or one-paragraph definition. (Nor, if you think about it, does journalism itself.) Even well-meaning journalists have been tempted to try to put it into a definitional box much too soon and too cozily based on one or more of its attributes or tools.

For example, several of the notable early experiments in public journalism employed, as one tool, surveys to discover citizens' concerns about their lives. Suddenly, in the minds of some journalists, public journalism became surveying, which sounded, to some, ominously like a marketing gimmick and to others like pandering to readers' desires.

It was as if investigative reporting suddenly was defined as "looking up records at the courthouse" because that is a tool it employs. The idea becomes captive of the tool and defined by it. Many tools exist for doing public journalism, but it is important at this early point that the tools not be used to define or limit the concept. Much more exploration needs to occur, unlimited by preconceptions.

It also needs to be understood that merely applying one or more of the tools or ideas does not turn otherwise routine work into public journalism, for example seeking the views of ordinary citizens on matters that affect them. Merely including those often-underinformed views in a newscast or story, as have some stations and newspapers, constitutes no more than a man-in-the-street interview; public journalism is purposefulness, not technique.

As the debate over public journalism swirled through the mid-1990s, the prevailing definitional anxiety and superficial understanding led to some strange exchanges with journalists who were interested in writing about public journalism, such as the following with a reporter from a large Eastern newspaper.

"I want to talk to you about public journalism."

"Sure, happy to," I said.

"Okay, now public journalism is where you write a story and show it to readers to see if it's alright to print, right?"

"Uh, I think we need a longer conversation."

With the foregoing experiences and caveats in mind, we can, for purposes of illustration, explore some tools and techniques. These few examples do not constitute a list; any list would be necessarily incomplete because public journalism is a work in progress. As more journalists understand the need to move beyond merely telling the news, they will invent their own tools and techniques. No claim of originality is made for the following tools and techniques; in many instances, it is not the technique that is new, it is the application of it in the context of engaging people in public life that makes it different.

The potential tools range from something as simple as a key paragraph in an otherwise traditional story to major, months-long reporting projects. It is not the occasional use of one or more of these tools that identifies an institution as doing public journalism; it is the consistent application of many of them over time so that the very nature of the journalism changes in subtle as well as obvious ways. For instance, a newspaper operating under public journalism principles would, over time, find that some stories that were important become less so, while others, ignored before, become part of the working definition of news. Such changes are subtle, and their effect can be measured only in whether public life in the community improves.

One additional caveat: as with any content choice, journalists can debate endlessly whether it was proper or the correct choice at that moment. These specific examples are cited not to invite debate on their appropriateness or perfection, but to show the kinds of things that need to be thought about and incorporated in experiments.

A DIFFERENT "NUT GRAF"

The concept of "the nut graf" is well entrenched in journalism. It is a paragraph high in the story that gets to the heart of the matter, succinctly adding broad perspective or context. Beyond the traditional informational uses of "nut grafs" lies the potential for more formative versions that can be useful in seeking to engage people more deeply. Such paragraphs stem from the reporter's human experience, reflecting not just the facts of the immediate situation but also known realities about how things work in the lives of people.

Two examples follow.

Choices Have Consequences

Far too often, even the best reporting loses sight of the fact that choices, political and otherwise, have consequences. The failure to relentlessly link choices and consequences in our reporting often leaves readers underinformed or puzzled about how things work—or don't work—or gives them a free pass from personal responsibility.

In late 1995, a Wichita woman shot and killed a boyfriend who had abused her over a period of time. Our reporting uncovered 19 arrest warrants outstanding for the man, Reggie Powell, most of them for abusing two women, including the woman who killed him, and for failing to show up for trials on those charges. Further checking revealed that the court involved had more than 125,000 unserved warrants for domestic abuse and similar crimes. All of this was occurring at a time of intense local and national concern over domestic abuse and also much furor about excessive taxes. Our reporting further indicated that the court's inability to keep up with all those warrants (and the people behind them) was due to an outdated and insufficient computer system. The system had not been upgraded because the officials involved were reluctant, in the hot antitax atmosphere, to ask for the millions required to do so. It was, by any measure, a compelling, disturbing story, but it got better, in public journalism terms. The lead of the story summarized the shooting, the tale of unserved warrants and habitual abusers going free, the details of the insufficient computer system, then came to this "nut graf:"

"Choices lie with the public. Accept the Reggie Powell syndrome as a way of life or pay for the (computer) fixes that are available for ... $3 million" ("Driven to Kill," *The Wichita Eagle,* Dec. 17, 1995, p. 1A).

One direct, simple paragraph, backed up with solid reporting, that illuminated the reality that choices have consequences and where those choices actually lie and whom the consequences ultimately affect. Without that paragraph and the reporting behind it, the problem would have been inaccurately and incompletely framed as a matter of an inept court system unable to keep up with the bad guys. With it, the consequences of alternative public choices were clear. The paragraph carefully did not suggest which choice might be preferable; that decision lay with citizens.

Targeting the Real Problem

For years, legislative bodies have struggled with the issue of campaign finance and how to reduce the influence of big money in elections. An accompanying public complaint revolves around what is seen as negative or attack campaigns, particularly on television. Stories about the problem routinely cite such facts as:

- A U.S. Senator must raise $18,000 a week, every week of his or her term, in order to be reelected.
- In an ironic reversal from years past, members of Congress now have a difficult time getting lobbyists on the telephone because the lobbyists know they are calling to solicit campaign contributions.
- The average Congressional campaign costs $500,000 and the typical Senate campaign $3.4 million.

As those stories are normally written, they focus attention on the antics officeholders go through to raise the money for reelection. Such framing allows readers to say, "Look at those jerks and what they do!" and retreat into their cocoon of cynicism and distrust.

There's a deeper and more pointed reality to that story. Senators must raise $18,000 a week and House candidates must struggle for money from lobbyists because they must buy television time. The reason they must buy television time, much of it for negative and attack advertising, is because it works. The candidate who spends the most money on television and who uses negative advertising almost always wins. The campaign finance dilemma is not simply a problem of people in Washington doing outrageous things; it is a public problem for which citizens, responding to the advertising, are as culpable as anyone else. Stories about campaign finance and abuses failing to make that clear are inaccurate and incomplete. Political campaigns will not stop doing the things that people claim to hate until those things no longer work, and only the public can make them no longer work.

BEYOND PARAGRAPHS

Story Framing

Journalists are story tellers. Whether the subject is a wreck on the highway or a major investigation, the story teller employs a narrative framework. The first content decisions involve an often-unconscious and reflex-based calculation: This story is about A and B, it is not about C, D, E, and F. Sometimes more thought leads to the inclusion of D or F, but at some point the frame and what's going to be in it are settled by a unilateral, subjective decision of the writer.

Rosen (1994b, Nov.) expressed the framing phenomenon this way:

Facts can't tell you how they want to be framed. Journalists decide how facts will be framed, and that means making decisions about which values will structure the story. We do not have a coherent philosophy that instructs the uncountable acts of framing that occur every day in journalism. What we have instead are certain rituals of framing—the way everyone does it. ... Becoming thoughtful about framing is central to what public journalism is about. ... What our philosophy says is that framing is not only an art—but one of the important democratic arts. (p. 8)

An example of framing choices:

A reporter notices that a large percentage of all prosecutions for cocaine and crack use are against African-Americans in a city in which the African-American population is less than 10%. His reporting tells him that usage is at least as high, percentage wise, among whites, and therefore the number of White users (and potential targets) is much higher than the number of African-American users. Further reporting points to some reasons for this: The crack trade in the African-American community is on the streets and in crack houses, whereas in the generally more affluent White community it is much less visible and thus much more expensive to attack; in poorer communities, people turn to other crimes to get money for drugs although more affluent people do not, which leads to more arrests in the poorer community for drug-related crimes; African Americans in this city tend to live in a concentrated geographic area whereas Whites, affluent or poor, are dispersed across the city—thus drug use is geographically more concentrated in the African-American community; citizens in the African-American community concerned about their neighborhoods have asked for, and received, more focused attention from police. Yet, without question, a larger number of Whites are using cocaine and crack than African-Americans.

Based on those facts, which can't tell you how they want to be framed, the reporter has choices.

One frame is to write that there is a defect in law enforcement that may be racially connected, or at least leaves that impression. In that frame, the picture that emerges is one of law enforcement at all levels focused inappropriately on African-Americans; it is a conflict-driven premise that can be supported by reaction quotes from police, prosecutors, and members of the African-American community who feel put upon. The uninvolved citizen, regardless of race, might have one or more conflicting reactions to such framing: Law enforcement has a problem that someone should address; the police are simply going where the crime is; law enforcement, with limited resources, can only pick targets of opportunity; somebody should stop selective enforcement because it is racist. All of those reactions place the problem somewhere else, implying that procedure or policy in law enforcement is the issue and that the answers lie in addressing those policies and procedures.

An alternative framing premise is that of a dilemma for the community rather than simply a defect in law enforcement. Such framing positions readers not as critics or spectators of a situation gone wrong but as stakeholders with an interest in things going right. In that frame, the picture that emerges is one of a community with an immediate problem (clearly, by the numbers, enforcement is not even-handed), but with larger challenges than that single symptom, such as housing patterns, law enforcement resources, and lack of community cooperation; it is a resolution-driven premise that can be supported by quotes from police, prosecutors, and members of the community about what things going right would be like and what is needed to help them go right. This framing would not ignore the symptom that gave rise to the reporting in the first place but would move beyond it, expanding the frame.

"Get With It" Information

Many newspapers and broadcast outlets occasionally tell people how to get involved in a discussion or a civic activity or respond to a need. This needs to be a daily habit relentlessly followed at every opportunity. It connects people with other people in many different ways and begins to define community in a different way. It's helpful, of course, if we also do occasional stories demonstrating the results of those connections. (See Success Stories, later this chapter.)

Making Ourselves Public

Some newspapers, including ours, list the reporter's beat and office telephone number at the end of every story. We encourage staffers to make themselves available for speaking to any group or gathering that requests it. There is, of course, a promotional aspect to these things, but the underlying reason is to allow people to see themselves as part of a public process of discussion and sharing information.

Identifying Stakeholders

Akin to story framing but more targeted is the idea of identifying the real stakeholders in a situation and making them central to the reporting and narrative. Doing that seems obvious and just good journalism, but it is amazing how many stories not only fail to recognize all stakeholders but often miss the central ones. For instance, most stories about schools and school policy revolve around school boards, administrators and teachers. Sometimes parents, who are also stakeholders, are included, but rarely are the ultimate stakeholders, the students, heard or seen, and when they are, their inclusion is often anecdotal and only incidental to the framing rather than integral to it.

It can be tempting to begin the search for stakeholders with the question, "Who are the potential winners and losers in this situation?" That's a false road to start down. Putting the question that way assumes that people are going to be acted on—turned into winners and losers—rather than be actors themselves. The purpose of identifying stakeholders is to include the voices of those stakeholders in the discussion before a decision that makes winners and losers is made.

Sometimes the ultimate stakeholders in a situation know they are just that even if we do not, and when our reporting fails to acknowledge their stake, they dismiss it as uninformed. At other times, ultimate stakeholders don't realize their stake unless we make it clear. Either way, clearly figuring out who all the stakeholders are and including them in the story is a reflex worth cultivating.

Exploring Core Values

Chapter 8 dealt with the value of values in journalism and the risks of our failure to recognize how people's core values affect their view of the world, driving the opinions they hold and the decisions they make. Before important issues can be resolved, competing core values must be resolved. It is possible for journalism to play a role in that process through directly addressing the values issue and helping readers understand that others may hold core values different from theirs—at times, directly competing values.

For instance, on the issue of building a new prison. One core belief is that the purpose of prison is to punish. A competing core belief is that the purpose of prison is to rehabilitate. The sort of prison built and the way it is operated depends largely on which core value prevails. Usually, the result is a compromise; neither core value is ignored and the outcome recognizes some aspects of each value. Our reporting needs to reflect those underlying beliefs as part of the discussion about what to do.

On many issues, it is useful to explore some of those core values to show how they relate to alternative public choices. In 1996, Wichita was struggling with the question of what to do about solid waste; whether to build a new landfill or a much more expensive transfer station to ship the waste elsewhere. The city had purchased land for a landfill, but nearby residents objected to it being built next door. We offered an exploration of some of the competing values that needed to be resolved and the implications of decisions based on those values:

- Personal property rights (no landfill over neighborhood objections) against meeting public, social needs (the trash must be dealt with).

- The local environment (no landfill) against cost factors (the transfer station is much more expensive).
- Accepting an obligation to solve our own waste problem (landfill) against shipping it elsewhere (transfer station).
- Maintaining political and social unity of the entire community by resolving the issue (landfill) against the disadvantages to a relatively few people.

One would favor one option over the other depending on which core value dominates. Directly outlining the competing core values and their implications allows people to understand choices and their consequences, to see their values as legitimate while understanding that others hold competing values, and to recognize that arriving at a resolution will necessarily involve, in Briand's words, "a shared conclusion about what is best, all things considered and in the circumstance for everyone" (1994, p. 17).

Success Stories

The dicey (for journalists) subject of success stories came up in a conversation with a couple of thirtyish reporters.

"The problem with success stories," one complained, "is that they're, well, they're just not interesting."

I waited a few seconds.

"To whom?" I asked.

A few more seconds passed.

"Well, they're just not interesting to ME," he said, blushing.

He had it right. Story ideas about things going well are as welcome in most newsrooms as a doubling of the price of coffee in the vending machine. They invariably are shoved at the least experienced reporter and shuffled to the back of local sections or zoned editions. Readers, on the other hand, like them and can learn from them, particularly if the reporter is skilled enough to get at underlying matters such as motivation.

Every journalist of any experience has tucked away in memory at least one anecdote about a story of success being printed, or almost printed, when suddenly the bottom falls out, or the executive skips town with the money. The risk of appearing naive or being taken outweighs, for many journalists, the usefulness of such stories. A result of this risk-aversion is that the picture we reflect back to people is not the picture they see through their own eyes. They recognize, and are interested in, successes; when we fail to report success as relentlessly and thoroughly as we report failure, we present a distorted picture of reality.

Advancing Deliberation

Yankelovich's exploration (see chapter 6, this volume) of how large issues are finally resolved by the public suggests a set of tools that journalists can use to help the move toward resolution. In *Coming to Public Judgment* (1991), he outlined 10 rules for resolution that leaders can use to speed the movement from mere opinion to true judgment that must occur before difficult issues are settled.

They include such things as "Give the public the incentive of knowing that someone is listening ... and cares" and " ... take the initiative in highlighting the values components of choices." With some modifications, his 10 rules offer ways that journalists can raise the level of discussion of critical issues and move it toward resolution by the public (pp. 160–176).

Major Projects

Major reporting projects have long been a part of journalism, and the first applications of public journalism techniques were in projects. The future of public journalism lies in our learning to apply the philosophy daily and weekly, but because projects are a part of the journalistic mix, they are included as a tool.

A public journalism project must be seen as such from the very conception of the idea. Trying to apply public journalism principles only in the writing will not work; it must begin with the concept and the basic reporting because applying public journalism principles presents an additional set of questions. For instance, a staff doing a project on a community problem would traditionally ask itself such questions as, "Is the reporting we have done accurate, complete, fair, thorough?" It would explore such questions as, "Why does the problem exist/persist; what mechanisms exist to deal with it; why are they not working?" Yet it also might ask itself an additional set of questions and do the reporting to answer these: What would be, in the broadest sense, good outcomes? What is the goal? What mechanisms—government, private, public—might come into being to help attack the problem? In other words, what capacity to deal with this problem is missing in public life, and how can that capacity be built and maintained? Who needs to talk with whom (and about what) to resolve the problem? What core values stand in the way of resolution and how and where can they be discussed?

That level of questioning and reporting, however, will not occur unless the journalists thinking about the issue have adopted a purpose beyond telling the news.

Something to Think About

Critics seeing the above list are quick to challenge, "There's nothing new about that. It's just good journalism." If that's the case, why isn't it being done? If "good journalism" is so obvious and easy, what is it about our culture that keeps us from doing it?

TWELVE

Cyberspace: Finding Our Way

Somewhere down the Information Superhighway lives Harold, the Rutabaga Man. He's not a bad sort, just overly internalized. Harold cares only about rutabagas, and he cares intensely about them, everything having to do with them: their history, how to cultivate them, cook them, their genetic composition, and their role in various cultures. It is his singular concern and passion as he sits in his cubicle with its electronic tentacles reaching anywhere in the universe. Empowered by modems, bemuscled with gigabytes, his blood hot with the power of interconnectivity, he can know anything known to humanity.

The technology that provides Harold's unbridled intellectual reach, however, also provides his personal opiate, for Harold is in sole command of the information he sees, and he wants to know only about rutabagas. Because he wills it, nothing else can impinge on his consciousness; he controls the keyboard and modem. The problem is, Harold can vote. Wouldn't probably, but could.

Harold and his cyberspace friends will redefine community, and perhaps democracy. Each is in electronic touch with a handful of similarly obsessed brothers and sisters, but there is no whole. By realizing their dreams of self-interest, they have fulfilled public life's most horrific nightmare.

Yet even worse, suppose that Harold's world is not the Information Superhighway and its already cliched spaghetti mix of off-ramps, on-ramps, and rest stops. That widely accepted metaphor of the information future is disarmingly comforting, for it implies a universe in which routes are clearly marked, directions are two-dimensional, and destinations are obtainable if only we follow the map properly from Point A to Point B. It is a technocrat's vision of people zipping confidently along predetermined routes to predetermined places.

131

Suppose, as seems more likely, the information future turns out to be an ocean; a broad, deep mass of molecular facts supplied by countless independent and unaccountable tributaries. It is suddenly three-dimensional, not two, and it is dark and cold at the bottom. The molecules of information that comprise it mingle together in a brew that is undrinkable when undiluted. It has currents not detectable to the unwary eye; great storms generated by the clashing of currents of dissimilar temperatures; a relentless natural food chain from which no creature is independent; no signposts and topography to provide safe navigation. If the Information Superhighway creates demassified chaos, how much more daunting will be the Information Ocean? How, in that muddled tracklessness, can the critical mass of shared information necessary to public life be assembled? Who will chart the vastness? Can communities be formed consisting of citizens able to act in democratic concert? Can democracy survive studied insularity? How can shared relevance, an essential element of democratic decision making, insinuate itself into Harold's new world? The questions are plump with implications for conscientious citizens and for journalists.

ALTERNATIVE FUTURES

There can be, of course, alternative futures in cyberspace, futures in which broader communities are formed. How those communities form, what they value, how broad they are, and what information they employ are all crucial issues for the intertwined futures of journalism and public life, for, as Fowler (1991) wrote, "The meaning of community is elusive, a word without an essence or a text without meaning," but "the concept ... invariably invokes the notion of commonality, of sharing in common, of being and experiencing together" (p. 3).

In a cyberspace world where geography—physical proximity—need not be a component of community, "experiencing together" necessarily implies the exchange of relevant information. The more persistent that exchange, the more vigorous the dialogue and the more relevant the information, the more likely that community is to thrive. Compelling evidence of this, and of journalism's stake in the proposition, can be found in Putnam's (1993) remarkable study of local government reform in Italy over two decades.

He and some associates were in Italy in 1970 when the Italian central government decided to reinvent the local governments in the country's 20 regions. Each region began with the same resources under the same set of rules. Putnam and his associates watched what happened over the next 20 years and, in 1993, published a landmark analysis that, among other things, clearly demonstrated the importance of journalism in successful communities and the importance to journalism of a vigorous civic life.

Over those two decades, not surprisingly, differences began to emerge among the reformed regions; some prospered economically more than others; some of the newly established governments were effective, some were not. The quality of life, measured in standard ways such as cultural and educational levels, was substantially better in some regions than in others, despite their even start in 1970.

Geography appeared to play no significant role, nor did pre-1970 history. What, then, made the difference? The Putnam group's careful analysis of sociological factors identified four predictors of success. Two of the strongest predictors of success are of particular interest here: (a) civic involvement; that is, the level of citizen activity in social, cultural, political, and sports organizations; and (b) newspaper reading. Again we see the strong connection between public life and journalism, their interdependence and joint importance in a successful community.

Stamm (1985) had earlier established a similarly clear connection. Based on extensive surveying and interviews, he concluded that people who feel connected to their communities tend to read newspapers (that is, consume journalism) at a higher rate than people who do not, and the reverse is also true: People who read newspapers tend to be connected to their communities.

Stamm's study was of cohesive geographic communities, but his lesson has been largely ignored by journalists despite its obvious important implications for both communities and journalism. If, for whatever reason, so clear cut a proposition does not become a factor in how journalists perform their jobs, what can be expected when communities, the "being and experiencing together," are tied more to affinity and interest than to geography and thus become much harder to define and cover?

DIFFERENT COMMUNITIES

Reporter (he prefers that title to critic or researcher) Joel Garreau (1991) explored that territory in *Edge City*, his term for the new frontier of American community: the office building-shopping mall-residential developments where a majority of Americans now live and that contain two thirds of the nation's office space. They are "third wave" communities. The first wave was the move from cities to the suburbs, mostly after World War II. The second was the movement of marketplaces toward where people lived—the "malling of America" trend of the 1960s and 1970s.

"Today," he observed, "we have moved our means of creating wealth, the essence of urbanism—our jobs—out to where most of us have lived and shopped for two generations. That has led to the rise of Edge City" (p. 4).

As cultural, religious, recreational, and intellectual activities were transferred to Edge City, a new array of associations was formed. Here, Garreau (1991) pointed out:

> You are no longer forced to proclaim your identity as part of any inexorable membership in a larger whole. You must find in yourself a reason to create a bond with other humans. ... Peer groups—community—are defined by job, avocation, church, or some other institution, far more than by location. ... [In Edge City] the main idea behind community is voluntary association, not geography. (pp. 278–279)

The differences between these new associations and traditional political, civic, and service organizations are profound. The new associations tend to be specific in aim and, therefore, are often transient. Reflecting the age, they tend to serve the inward, personal needs of people rather than a larger, generalized public or political need.

Often they attract victims or potential victims of what they see as threatening: antitaxers, militant pro-lifers, gun ownership pro-and-conners, neighborhood watchers. Others are bound by affinity: joggers, parapsychologists, tree huggers, horse owners, cat haters, lefthanders, rutabaga lovers, stamp collectors, video gamers, poets, golfers, marrieds, unmarrieds, wannabe marrieds, parents without partners, and partners without parents. Think of a human fear, activity, or proclivity and there is an association—and perhaps a foundation—that ties people together in its cause.

These affinity associations can be viewed as falling into two broad categories: those that participate vigorously in, and often frame, political and social debate, and those that operate outside the public sphere, in self-selected privacy. Both kinds are worth the close attention of journalists. The manic networking is fueled by the communications revolution that provides faxes, modems, bulletin boards, electronic publishing, tapes, videos, and, of course, newsletters; no need for clubhouses and face-to-face meetings; no agendas except the foundational one; no charters and rules save mutual interest.

Rheingold (1993) debated with himself whether:

> Cyberspace is one of the informal public places where people can rebuild the aspects of community that were lost when the malt shop became a mall. Or perhaps cyberspace is precisely the wrong place to look for a rebirth of community, offering not a tool of conviviality but a life-denying simulacrum of real passion and true commitment to one another. In either case, we need to find out soon. (p. 26)

For journalists, and for democracy's future, this poses a huge problem. In an Edge City society in which associations of affinity are not related to geography, how will those nascent communities organize and communicate the shared information required for the "experiencing together" of democracy? Will they, in their many and varied forms and interests, somehow constitute a democratic whole, or will Postman's (1985) neighborhood of strangers expand to include everyone? Clearly journalists have a stake in the answers unless we are satisfied with the prospect of being mere information providers in a universe full of information providers.

An understanding of the role of journalism in creating operational publics is hardly new. Tocqueville (1990) reported on it in his revelatory tour of the United States in 1831 and 1832:

> Nothing, in my opinion, is more deserving of our attention than the intellectual and moral associations of America. ... (p. 110)

> Americans of all ages, all conditions, and all dispositions constantly form associations ... of a thousand ... kinds, religious, moral, serious, futile, general or restricted, enormous or diminutive. The Americans make associations to give entertainments, to found seminaries, to build inns, to construct churches, to diffuse books, to send missionaries to the antipodes; in this manner they found hospitals, prisons and schools. ... If it is proposed to inculcate some truth or to foster some feeling by encouragement of a great example, they found a society. (pp. 106–107)

The relentless formation of associations, he decided, sprang out of the notion of equality. In a democracy, "They all become powerless if they do not learn voluntarily to help one another" (p. 107). He also understood the connection between associations and the journalism of that day:

> To suppose that [newspapers] only serve to protect freedom would be to diminish their importance: they maintain civilization. ... In democratic countries ... it frequently happens that a great number of men who wish or want to combine cannot ... because they are very insignificant and lost in the crowd, they cannot see and do not know where to find one another. ... The newspaper brought them together, and the newspaper is still necessary to keep them united. (pp. 111–112)

In the electronic future, journalists will have to become adept at making things rather than simply finding things, to use Rosen's (1993) formulation:

> This always confuses [my students] because everything they have been told states that journalists are people who find things—stories, facts, news. If journalists do, in fact, make things, then their field is an art, not

a science. We might say that journalism is one of the more important arts of democracy, and its ultimate purpose is not to make news, or reputations, or headlines, but simply to make democracy work.

IN SEARCH OF A FUTURE ROLE

Some points to consider about the role of journalism in cyberspace include:

- Competition: A portion of what is now considered "journalistic product" because it is conveyed in newspapers and by broadcast will be up for grabs. People who now pay newspapers to organize and deliver to them certain kinds of data will have other options. Stock markets, financial reports, weather, sports scores, even police calls and court cases and such government-originated information will be available either directly from the sources or from other information-gathering entities. The latter will have a financial advantage over traditional news organizations because they will not have the overhead of journalistic organizations.
- Revenue: That overhead disadvantage arises from the costs incurred to add certain values to the commodity of raw data: perspective, context, cohesion—in a word, usefulness. A crucial question for journalism in the electronic future is how does a journalistic organization (as opposed to a data-gathering one) get paid for adding that value, particularly if it is not able to offset the cost of adding value by also being paid for providing the raw data?
- Revenue sources: In 1994, newspapers derived roughly 80% of their revenue from advertising, 20% from circulation; television gets virtually all of its revenue from advertising—that money supports its news products. In an interactive media world where people need be exposed only to what they choose, how will advertisers ensure that their messages will be seen? Will advertising become indistinguishable from news, or built into it, breaking down that important journalistic wall between the two? What will that do to journalistic credibility? Will advertising develop its own cyberspace, relying on people's legitimate informational needs to gain exposure? If that happens, where will the revenue come from to support the news products thus abandoned by advertising? One implication of the last possibility is forbidding for a democracy: If journalism loses its advertising revenue base, it must then charge much more for access to news, thereby making it an elitist product accessible to relatively few.

- Audience: Given the myriad of informational options and the implications of the revenue question, how does a journalistic institution identify and organize its audience, let alone turn that audience into a public?

TECHNOLOGY IS NOT ENOUGH

A group of journalists, academics, and foundation people concerned with such questions gathered at Harvard University's Nieman Foundation in the spring of 1994 to begin worrying the subject. Andrew Blau (1994), director of the Benton Foundation's communications policy project, outlined the challenges thus:

> Journalism in the electronic future will be under pressure at four of its most important strong points. Journalism organizes the universe of possible information; it arbitrates the truth or importance of that information; it organizes a public out of the universe of people who could be dealing with that information; and it generates money to pay journalists for the value they add to raw information.

All of these, he contends, "are being radically undermined by what's happening" in cyberspace. In the electronic future:

> There is no automatic setting for creating and presenting a point of view. Because creating cohesion, context, or a point of view is what journalists do, that setting must somehow be established, and there is no template for it. Given that, how does a public become organized? How can journalism cut through the other noise in cyberspace? Given those circumstances, how do you get paid for adding value to the universe of possible information?

As expected, this first Nieman session raised many questions and answered none, but it was the beginning of a serious search for a journalistic foothold in the future. My concern about that future goes beyond even Blau's (1994) discomforting formulation. If the value added is only cumulative, only additional levels of complexity and subtlety, the underlying problems of journalism and public life are not eased.

Assume for a moment that existing news organizations or their immediate progeny successfully transplant themselves into the cyberspace future. Suppose (against all the indications of recent history) those companies are there first and are positioned to be paid for fulfilling both the basic informational needs and the added journalistic values, the context and point of view. Suppose the horror of Harold the Rutabaga Man is somehow avoided. If nothing else changed, we would merely be transplanting into the information future the same untrusted product, and that would be no more sufficient in cyberspace than it is in the mid-1990s on newsprint and over the airwaves.

So solving the tremendous technical, competitive, marketing, and organizational challenges of the electronic future guarantees nothing either to journalism or to public life. The real value that journalists can and must take into the future is purposefulness, demonstrating to an introverted citizenry both the usefulness and the necessity of shared relevance to the democratic process. That means adopting as a goal the identification and cultivation of communities and the creation of methods where shared relevance can be put to use by those communities. It means regaining lost institutional trust and authority through important cultural change.

Merely telling the news the same way in bytes and bits instead of by mouth and type may keep some form of journalism alive for a while, but unless that journalism finds a more secure connection with citizens and their concerns and recognizes its obligation to public life, it, too, will pass.

THIRTEEN

So What's It All About?

I call the ideas that I have been expressing public journalism. Others call it civic or community journalism. Still others, contending that there's nothing new in the philosophy, call it "just good journalism." The name and its characterization as new or old are matters of indifference to me. Old or new, public or civic, or "just good ... ," it is not being done now, and it needs to be.[1]

Public journalism moves beyond current practice by adopting a particular, pragmatic view of the nature of democracy and the role of journalism in it. That view of democracy holds that although our system is representative rather than direct, the people cannot and do not give away ultimate power; we lend portions of it to chosen representatives. The only way for people to retain their ultimate power is by being engaged in its exercise. That view leads to a conviction, and a resultant attitude, about the relationship between journalism and public life: that journalism has a role beyond telling the news, beyond the mere provision of information.

Therefore, public journalism involves these mental shifts:

- It moves beyond the limited mission of telling the news to a broader mission of helping public life go well, and acts out of that imperative.

  When public life goes well, true deliberation occurs and leads to potential solutions.
- It moves from detachment to being a fair-minded participant in public life.

  Its practitioners remember that they are citizens as well as journalists, stakeholders in a process that needs their presence.

---

[1]Portions of this chapter first appeared in "Missing the Point," *American Journalism Review*, July/August 1996.

- It moves from worrying about proper separations to concern with proper connections.

  If we get the proper connections right, the separations will take care of themselves.
- It moves beyond only describing what is going wrong to also imagining what going right would be like.

  By describing realistic possibilities that lie beyond immediate responses to problems, it informs people of their potential choices for the future.
- It moves from seeing people as consumers—as readers or non-readers, as bystanders to be informed—to seeing them as a public, as potential actors in arriving at democratic solutions to public problems.

  It therefore relentlessly seeks ways to encourage public involvement and true deliberation; ways to build the public capacity to talk about and form solutions.

Journalists must explore the rich ground individually, using the mental shifts already described to define public journalism by their individual consciences and judgments and the needs of their communities. The "why," the thrust of the idea, however, is to move journalism beyond telling the news to a more purposeful and socially useful goal of helping public life go well. This does not mean ceasing to tell the news in the myriad ways that journalism's useful, if peculiar, culture dictates. Public journalism is additive. It builds on telling the news by recognizing (a) the fundamental connection between democracy and journalism, (b) the need for public life to go well, for democracy to fulfill its historic promise, and (c) journalism's rational self-interest, both economic and intellectual, in public life's going well.

The price of failing to take those realities into account is high: If citizens continue to leave public life to the professionals and experts who are all too willing to have it to themselves, they have no need of journalism or journalists. In the long run, the democratic system will founder.

The hope of reinvolving a broad range of citizens in public life lies in how issues and information are presented in the first instance; that is, on the front page and at the top of the newscast. That's when people face an immediate question of whether the issue or information is important (useful, interesting, threatening) to them and whether they can hope to affect the circumstances being described.

Theoretically in a democracy, it is almost always possible to answer "yes" to those questions, but the answers heard today are almost always "no." That resignation, that abandonment of hope arises because the conventions of telling the news do not allow journalists to pose the questions in a way that makes "yes" easier. The promise of public journalism lies in giving citizens that access, that insight. This is not a matter of contrivance; it is a matter of focused attention to and accurate reporting of the whole range of possibilities implicit in any situation.

Public journalism is not easy; if it were, it wouldn't be particularly important or particularly interesting; it would merely be a different, if controversial, journalistic technique. It is much more than technique. It requires a philosophical journey because it is a fundamental change in how we conceive of our role in life.

The magnitude of that change is akin to the shift in the practice of medicine, an analogy first expressed by Rosen (1994, Nov.). Thirty or so years ago, he pointed out, if you were well, the medical profession had no particular interest in you. Doctors treated disease, and most people's encounters with the profession began with the need for immediate attention to a problem. A few thoughtful doctors, weary perhaps of dealing only in the disease mode and often treating clearly preventable illnesses, began to wonder if it might be more useful to devote time and resources to preventing disease in the first place. The idea, being fresh, was not without its detractors in the profession, some of whom considered intervention in the lives of well people as unwarranted intrusion, even self-pro-motional. The reformers eventually prevailed, although the shift in point of view, elegant in its simplicity, took decades to complete. Few would now disagree that the profession and the public are better for the change from treating disease to preventing its occurrence. Treating disease is still a vital and honored part of medicine. It has not been replaced, it has been supplemented.

As with medicine of decades ago, much of journalism still operates on the disease model, and will always need to do so. However, some journalists who view their role as potentially more useful than only dealing with society's ills are thinking about ways to help prevent those illnesses in the first place. It is an intellectual journey not unlike that taken by the medical profession.

The first two steps on that journey are:

- Acceptance of the fact that, whether we like it or not or are comfortable with it, journalism in the media age is an integral part of the system of public life, an active, even if reluctant, participant in it. In a word, journalists are unavoidably "players", even though our proper role is not to be partisan or political in the traditional sense.
- Recognition that journalism's integral role in public life imposes an obligation on us. The obligation is to do our journalism in ways that are calculated to help public life go well by reengaging people

in it. Public life "going well" means that democracy succeeds in answering its core question: What shall we do? The answer, in a democracy, should be found by informed and engaged citizens. (Another way of putting this is building civic capital, a residue of public knowledge and experience in the art of democracy.) Public journalism does not seek to forge its own answer to the core question "What shall we do?" It actively seeks to help citizens arrive at their answer.

I believe that the first point is inarguable, for to deny it is to deny that journalism is of any consequence whatsoever, which in turn would raise the question "Why do it?"

The second point is the point of departure, for it requires a step away from traditional journalistic detachment. It calls for a purposefulness and declared intent as we go about our work. It is precisely at this point that much concern and some confusion arises. Most journalists hear the critique of detachment and take not a step but a mental leap: If we're not talking about detachment, they say, then we must be talking about attachment; and if we're talking about attachment, then we must be talking about abandoning such indisputably important and useful roles as watchdog, outsider from government, independent observer, uninvolved-and-thus-credible source of information.

Public journalism and those traditional ideals are neither in conflict nor mutually exclusive. Public journalism adds to those ideals an additional imperative: concern for whether citizens become engaged in public life. If people are not engaged, democracy fails; and if people are not engaged in public life, they have no need for journalists or journalism.

Public journalism has been called "solutions journalism," but it is not aimed at solving problems; it is aimed at reengaging citizens in solving problems. It does not seek to join with or substitute itself for government (in either case an outrageous and impossible aspiration); it seeks to keep citizens in effective contact with the governing process. Its goal is not to better connect journalists with the community, but to better connect the people in communities with one another. So it is as much or more about public life than it is about journalism.

In this respect, it is regrettable that public journalism was first expressed in large-scale projects. Those early projects gained some considerable attention, which led to the wrong questions being asked. The question from ever-pragmatic journalists was always *How* did you do that? rather than the more pertinent and foundational *Why* did you do that?

The "how" answers focused the attention on technique, leading to mimicking of the "how" without regard for the required understanding of "why?" Lets be clear about this: It's silly—and dangerous—to set out to "do public journalism" simply because that's what some people are doing, or that's what the boss said, or that's one of our newsroom goals this year. If you don't get it philosophically, you will not get it right.

The project-oriented beginning, although perhaps unavoidable (and at any rate a fact), masked the underlying principles and delayed the idea's maturation. The useful future of public journalism is not in major projects, as important as they are, but in our learning to use daily and weekly an additional set of reflexes. The way we now do routine reporting systematically discourages people about public life, including politics. *Learning* is an important word here because no one really knows how to do that yet; it's an unfulfilled intellectual and occupational challenge.

IF NOT JOURNALISTS, WHO?

The inescapable question that public journalism chooses to address rather than avoid is: If not us, who? In the dynamic of people, public life, politics, and journalism, only journalism has the combination of complete freedom and potential power to define its role, to set its own goals, to act—within reason—as it wishes. For public journalists, that constitutionally protected freedom imposes a moral obligation (although certainly not a legal one) to act.

The political part of the dynamic is not going to change on its own. So long as elections are held and office and power gained, the winners will perpetuate the shoddy system because it works for them. The public yearns for change—believes it can happen—but that things are not getting better, in large part because politics and journalism cannot be trusted to help. That is a capacity problem. The public, in a democracy, can regain control, but the capacity to do it must first be rebuilt. Journalism can do that, over time.

STEPS FOR GETTING THERE

Time, however, may be an unaffordable luxury. When trust in journalism is halved in only 5 years, between 1988 to 1993, and only one in five people expresses great confidence in it, the last grains of sand are running rapidly. Public life and journalism did not reach their current states overnight; it took decades. It is arguable that we do not have decades for the repair work.

Moving the necessary change along requires the efforts of three groups of people: willing journalists, conscientious citizens, and journalism educators. The way for willing journalists to progress has been the subject of most of this book. We must be willing to challenge the axioms under which we have been nurtured and look for a more publicly useful way. Conscientious citizens and journalism educators must also be willing to challenge comfortable assumptions and take risks.

Some possible steps for educators:

1. Build into journalism curricula a deeply developed under-standing of how and why democracy does and does not work. This is beyond politics alone, and includes other aspects of public life, now and in the electronic future.

2. If necessary, substitute such courses for some of the technical courses that now consume students' limited time. One possible experi-ment: advanced journalism students might learn the technical aspects in real newsrooms at the same time they are building the necessary academic background in classrooms. This is an expansion of present intern programs, the difference being that the two would go on simultaneously. Internship programs are now limited by the resources of the newsrooms providing them. In this experiment, the students' tuitions would finance that part of his or her education as well as the academic part.

3. Build a mission into beginning reporting, writing and editing classes beyond merely processing information into news stories. The "H" of the traditional "Five W's and an H" (who, what, where, when, why, and how) needs to stand for not only how something occurred but for *handle*: ways that citizens can get their hands around a problem and help devise solutions.

4. Develop and encourage courses in media literacy for students in other disciplines to help them learn how information, including that provided by journalism, drives public life and how to be informed users of it.

5. Devote more faculty resources and energy to philosophical and qualitative explorations and, if necessary, less to trying to quantify those parts of journalism that are essentially unquantifiable, not worthy of such treatment, and yield only superficial value. Quantitative analysis has enormous value in journalism and journalism academics, both as a tool for greatly enriched reporting and as a way of finding out what works and what does not work in the making of effective content. Journalism is not a science, however, it is a human art. Although it is possible to measure almost everything, it does not automatically follow that attempting to quantify everything is the most useful application of limited resources.

Some steps for citizens:

1. Develop a keen sense of belonging, a concept expressed by Mathews (1994):

Behaving as though we belong is the way we act in our church or synagogue or at a reunion. We feel at home and act accordingly. We are aware of how our behaviors affect others, the place we are in and the place we want to maintain. No one has to tell us that. Yet, we take responsibility for the consequences of our actions in ways that we don't take in places where we don't think we belong. (p. 206)

2. Develop patience as a democratic skill, a concept expressed by Lappe and DuBois (1994):

As we develop a public life in which we work for ends we care about deeply, these painful truths—that life and social change can be deeply frustrating—require something deeper than ordinary patience. We need an appreciation of the unevenness of human growth. (pp. 289–290)

3. Be open to developing a new understanding of and relationship with "the media." Whether or not you like it, you have a stake in how journalists perform and in what they see as their job, because what they do is tied so closely to how public life proceeds. Look not simply for information but also for usefulness—if you do not find it, demand it. Allowing yourself to be turned away from public life because of a lack of useful information is too high a price.

To this end, a useful list of approaches is provided by Everette C. Dennis in his 1993 Roy Howard Lecture at Indiana University. His charge is that citizens can and should assert their influence over journalism. Among the ways he suggested doing this:

Being informed about media as they relate to daily life by being attentive to media coverage of media … ;

Talking back to the media by writing letters to the editor or by writing or calling electronic media station managers when you think something is wrong … ;

Writing and calling working reporters and producers who are on the firing line in producing news reports;

Urging organizations you belong to and institutions with which you are associated to be responsive to the media and to generate feedback;

Giving support to media literacy classes in schools;

Being conscious and self-conscious about media connections and influences so that you make sure you use the media for your edification rather than be used by them. (p. 17)

4. Do not give up. A well-developed sense of belonging, patience, and seeing journalism as a resource in a different way will ultimately pay off. As with all important change, however, this will not be easy.

Epilogue

February 1997. The journey continues. Since 1994, when I took a year's leave of absence from *The Eagle* to write the first edition of this book, much has changed. After returning to the editorship for 2 years, in January of 1997 I became Senior Editor, stepping aside from the day-to-day operations of the newspaper in order to spend full time talking, writing and thinking about public journalism.

Only rarely does a person receive the opportunity to indulge what has become a passion, but that opportunity is at hand. The epilogue to the first edition ended with these words: "Prove it? I cannot. But talk to me in 10 years." On some darker days, when critics of public journalism seem in the ascendancy, I think of that as overly optimistic. On other days, as I hear from journalists in this country and abroad who are thinking hard about the philosophy, I am heartened. The encouraging fact is that the critics have taken their best, or worst, shots yet the idea continues to grow and mature. If it is indeed a sound idea for journalism and democracy, it will live. If it is not, it will find some other form or, perhaps, simply become an artifact of the nation's and the profession's troubled times in the closing years of the 20th Century.

I am often asked: Why you? What caused you to take this step?

Libby would answer that more confidently than I. She believes that there are no coincidences; that good and bad things happen to people who make themselves available—or susceptible—to events by their own actions and instincts. My response would be somewhat less mystical and slightly more pragmatic: a confluence of time, place, and circumstance; an accumulation of blows, in boxing parlance. Whoever is right, this journey could not have started in New York or Los Angeles or Miami. It had to start in the heartland. In could not have started with any other newspaper company than Knight-Ridder, which is open to new thoughts and experimentation. It could not have started in 1965 or 1975 or 1985 (although I wish it had).

What now? What are the possibilities? Where does this lead? At any time in history many forces are at work, and although journalism is only one of the forces at work in our society today, it has unique potential to affect public life.

Journalism cannot create and solely sustain a healthy public life; only conscientious citizens and civic institutions can do that. But journalism that adopts a purpose beyond telling the news, that informs and reminds people of their potential, that reinforces the promise and responsibility inherent in a democratic society can be the gravity that keeps a wonderfully diverse and frustratingly contentious society together.

References

Barlett, D. L., & Steele, J. B. (1992). *America: What went wrong?* Kansas City, MO: Andrews & McMeel.

Blau, A. (1994, May). Panel discussion at the Foundation seminar, Harvard University, Cambridge, MA.

Breslow, P. (Senior Producer). (1994, May 14). *National Public Radio weekend edition.*

Briand, M. (1994). *Understanding deliberation.* New York: Project on Public Life and the Press.

Carey, J. F. (1974). Journalism and criticism: The case of an undeveloped profession. *The Review of Politics, 26,* 227–249.

Claiborne, J. (1986). *The* Charlotte Observer: *Its time and place.* Chapel Hill: University of North Carolina Press.

Dennis, E. (1993). *Fighting media illiterary: What every American needs to know* (Roy W. Howard Lecture, No. 4). Bloomington: Indiana University Press.

Dionne, E. J., Jr. (1992). *Why Americans hate politics.* New York: Touchstone Books.

Fowler, R. B. (1991). *The dance with community.* Lawrence: University of Kansas Press.

Garreau, J. (1991) *Edge city: Life on the new frontier.* New York: Anchor.

Hallin, D. C. (1992, Spring). Sound bite news: Television coverage of elections, 1968–1988. *Journal of Communication, 42,* 5–24.

Hunter, J. D. (1994). *Before the shooting begins.* New York: The Free Press.

Iyengar, S. (1991). *Is anyone responsible? How television frames political issues.* Chicago: University of Chicago Press.

Lambeth, E. B. (1986). *Committed journalism.* Bloomington: Indiana University Press.

Lappe, F. M., & DuBois, P. M. (1994) *The quickening of America.* San Francisco: Jossey-Bass.

Lippmann, W. (1965). *Public opinion.* New York: The Free Press.

Manchester, W. (1967). *The death of a president.* New York: Harper & Row.

Mathews, D. (1993, November). *Address to American Press Institute seminar,* Reston, VA.

Mathews, D. (1994). *Politics for people.* Chicago: University of Illinois Press.

Merritt, D. (1988, November 13). Must restore meaning to election camapigns. *Wichita Eagle,* p. 15A.

Merritt, D. (1990, September 9). Here's our election bias. *Wichita Eagle,* p. 13A.

National Broadcasting Company. (1966). *Seventy hours and thirty minutes.* New York: Random House.

Neuman, W. R., Just, M. R., & Crigler, A. N. (1992). *Common knowledge: News and the construction of political meaning.* Chicago: University of Chicago Press.

Page, B. and Shapiro, R. (1992). *The Rational Public.* Chicago: University of Chicago Press.

Postman, N. (1985). *Amusing ourselves to death.* New York: Penguin.

Putnam, R. (1993). *Making democracy work: Civic traditions in modern Italy.* Princeton, NJ: Princeton University Press.

Rheingold, H. (1993). *The virtual community.* Reading, MA: Addison-Wesley.

Rosen, J. (1993). Beyond objectivity. *Nieman Reports, 47*(4), 48–53.

Rosen, J. (1994a, March). *Getting the connections right.* Presentation to Project on Public Life and the Press, American Press Institute. Reston, VA.

Rosen, J. (1994b, November), *Public journalism as a democratic art.* Presentation to the Project on Public Life and the Press, American Press Institute. Reston, VA.

Silva, D. (Senior Producer). (1994, July 11). CNN Crossfire. Washington, DC: Cable News Network.

Smith, S. (1997). Getting down and dirty with the critics, *Civic Catalyst,* January 1997, Washington, D.C.: The Pew Center for Civic Journalism.

Squires, J. D. (1993). *Read all about it! The corporate takeover of America's newspapers.* New York: Times Books.

Stamm, K. R. (1985). *Newspaper use and community ties.* Norwood, NJ: Ablex.

Television news angers Reagan. (1982, March 17). *The Daily Oklahoman,* p. 1.

Time Magazine (1959). 77(2), 59.

Time Magazine (1984). 123(18), 62.

Times-Mirror Center for The People and The Press. (1994). *The people, the press & politics: The new political landscape.* Washington, DC: Author.

de Tocqueville, A. (1990). *Democracy in America.* New York: Vintage Classics.

Toffler, A. (1981). *The third wave.* New York: Bantam.

Weaver, D., & Wilhoit, G. C. (1992). *The American journalist in the 1990s.* Arlington, VA: The Freedom Forum.

Westbrook, R. (1991). *John Dewey and American democracy.* Ithaca: Cornell University Press.

Yankelovich, D. (1991). *Coming to public judgment.* Syracuse, NY: Syracuse University Press.

Index